The Vermont Gardener's Companion

Gardener's Companion Series

The Vermont
Gardener's Companion

*An Insider's Guide to Gardening in
the Green Mountain State*

Second Edition

Henry Homeyer

Globe
Pequot

Guilford, Connecticut

Globe Pequot

An imprint of Rowman & Littlefield

Distributed by NATIONAL BOOK NETWORK

Copyright © 2016 by Rowman & Littlefield

Illustrations by Josh Yunger
Map: M.A. Dubé © Rowman & Littlefield

British Library Cataloguing in Publication Information Available

Library of Congress Cataloging-in-Publication Data

Names: Homeyer, Henry, author.
Title: The Vermont gardener's companion : an insider's guide to gardening in the Green Mountain State / Henry Homeyer.
Other titles: Gardener's companion series.
Description: Second edition. | Guilford, Connecticut : Globe Pequot, [2016] | Series: Gardener's companion series | Includes index.
Identifiers: LCCN 2015038510| ISBN 9781493022113 (pbk. : alk. paper) | ISBN 9781493022120 (e-book)
Subjects: LCSH: Gardening--Vermont.
Classification: LCC SB453.2.V5 H66 2016 | DDC 635.09743--dc23 LC record available at http://lccn.loc.gov/2015038510

∞™ The paper used in this publication meets the minimum requirements of American National Standard for Information Sciences—Permanence of Paper for Printed Library Materials, ANSI/NISO Z39.48-1992.

For my granddaughter, Casey Jean-Marie Yunger,
born March 25, 2007. I waved snowdrops under your nose when you
were just a few hours old . . . and you opened your eyes.

Contents

Introduction

Welcome to the second edition of *The Vermont Gardener's Companion*. In the eight years since this book was first printed, I have crisscrossed the state giving talks to garden clubs, library groups, and Master Gardeners. I met many gardeners, both new and experienced. Based on that experience I decided to add two chapters to this new edition. I have also updated and added paragraphs throughout the book. Just like your computer, your gardening reference needs updating from time to time.

The first new chapter is called Eating from the Garden All Year—which is something I do. As I traveled around the state, many gardeners expressed an interest in learning the best ways to freeze, dehydrate, and store the bounty of the vegetable garden. It's not rocket science; anyone can do it. I'll share my tricks you.

The other new chapter, Tools of the Trade, reviews the tools needed by gardeners and describes how to use them effectively while avoiding a sore back. It explains why one type of wheelbarrow, for example, might be perfect for you—but maybe not for your mom. Or why one weeding tool might be just right for getting out creeping grass roots.

Gardeners in Vermont regularly overcome some pretty big challenges: winter temperatures that plunge far below zero; rocks left behind by glaciers that pop out of the ground each spring like bread from hyperactive toasters; and the usual medley of bugs and diseases that plague gardeners throughout the Northeast. Despite all that, Vermont gardeners prevail, harvesting wonderful veggies, fruits, and flowers. This book is designed to make your efforts more rewarding and your life as a gardener a little easier.

From the outset I must make a confession: I'm not a Vermonter. I live about 5 miles into foreign territory: across the Connecticut River in New Hampshire. I like to joke that when I bought my house in Cornish Flat back in 1970 I thought I was moving to

Vermont—and that I only figured out that I hadn't when I saw the slogan "Live Free or Die" on my license plate.

Although I'm not a Vermonter, I spend a lot of time in Vermont and feel at home in Vermont. My stepson, Josh Yunger, who illustrated this book, lives in South Strafford with his wife, Erin, and my grandchildren, George and Casey, whom I visit often. I was the Vermont associate editor of *People, Places, and Plants* magazine for 10 years, so I traveled all over the state to interview gardeners. I write a weekly newspaper column that appears in papers around the state, and I am a regular commentator on gardening for Vermont Public Radio.

This book will offer you some advice about how to garden in the Green Mountain State and how to get the most out of its short gardening season. I'm an organic gardener, so if you're looking for suggestions about what synthetic chemicals to spray on your roses or broccoli, this is not the book for you. But I will share with you some of what I've learned in more than fifty years of organic gardening, such as how I deal with pests.

I started gardening in the early 1950s when my maternal grandfather, John Lenat, introduced me to the joys of playing with water and dirt, of studying earthworms, and of eating ripe red tomatoes warmed by the summer sun. He didn't care if I got dirty, and he never complained if I just wanted to listen to his stories while he worked—instead of weeding. I loved being with him, and he taught me to love the garden.

Grampy was an organic gardener long before it was popular. He made compost and worked it into his beds when other home gardeners were extolling the virtues of chemical fertilizers—the so-called modern way to garden. We brought home buckets of chicken manure from the local egg farm, and he let me make "tea" for our tomatoes in an old wooden rain barrel. He picked off voracious bugs and put them in soapy water instead of spraying chemicals, a technique I still use.

I own just a couple of acres and live in an old wooden house built as the Cornish Creamery in 1888. I have good soil, a small stream, and all the basic growing conditions one could want: full sun to full shade, wet to dry . . . and everything in between. And I am obsessed with trying to grow everything—from apples, artemisias, and artichokes to wildflowers, yuccas, and zucchinis.

It's my belief that gardening nourishes and strengthens not only the body (with fresh vegetables and hard work), it nurtures the soul. Had a hard day at work? Mad at (you pick) your teenager, boss, or the neighbor's ill-mannered dog? Get out in the garden. Pull weeds. Better yet, plant something. There is a primal urge wired into most of us to plant things. Plant a six-pack of annual flowers or a few pumpkin seeds and you'll feel better. Or pick some flowers and arrange them in a vase. You will feel like a new person, only vaguely resembling the ogre who walked down to the garden.

Gardening is not all success, of course. Years ago striped cucumber beetles used to eat my cukes when they were in the two-leafed stage, gnawing them down to the ground. So I'd replant. And replant until the weather changed or the beetles found something tastier. Some years I didn't get very many cucumbers because it was July before the plants got established, but I refused the "nuclear option"—pesticides. Then I learned about row covers. By stretching a layer of a thin agricultural fabric known as Reemay over the hill, I was able to physically prevent the beetles from getting to my plants. No poisons and plenty of organic cucumbers. My goal is to help you deal with some of the challenges facing gardeners who reject toxic chemicals.

This guide to gardening in Vermont is primarily based on methods that I have tried and found to work. It also contains information I have learned from scientists and gardeners who have researched aspects of gardening outside my areas of expertise. But I've tried to keep the book user friendly: I kept the science simple and provided information that has real hands-on benefit to you, the gardener. Thus, for example, I will share with you what research is going on to find nontoxic ways to control the lily leaf beetle (that gorgeous red terrorist that is devastating lilies in parts of the Green Mountain State). Or what can be done about purple loosestrife, the purple flower that is taking over our wetlands. If I have used a word you don't know, you should find it defined in the glossary at the back of the book.

The University of Vermont has wonderful resources for gardeners through UVM Extension and the UVM Horticultural Research Center outside of Burlington. This book will help you connect with them. I have interviewed teachers at UVM to get Vermont-specific information. The resource section in the back of the book will give you websites and phone numbers of Vermonters who can help you, as well as sources for purchasing seeds, tools, and biological controls of pests. My favorite gardening books are back there, too.

From information about lawns and lilies, to mulches and mole repellent, this book will provide useful information for Vermont gardeners. Gardening should be fun, and I hope this book will also entertain you as you settle in by the woodstove in midwinter or into an Adirondack chair in the shade on a hot summer afternoon.

Henry Homeyer

Firm
Foundations

CHAPTER ONE

Soils

More than anything else, being a successful gardener depends on having good soil. Green thumbs? Malarkey. No such thing. Good soil is what counts the most. Want to grow peonies or blueberries? You'll need to do more than just dig a small hole and plunk in a plant if you expect to have success. This chapter explains the basics of soils and what you can do to improve yours—and make it suitable for the plants you want to grow. Vermont soils vary considerably from the rich loam of the Connecticut River Valley to the rocky soils of the Green Mountains and the clays along Lake Champlain. But an understanding of how soils work, and what yours is like, will serve you well.

What's in Your Vermont Soil?

Soils are composed of three things: first, ground-up rocks that were largely created when the glaciers churned their way across Vermont and then retreated 10,000 years ago, grinding mountains into molehills—and into sand, silt, and clay. Running water and today's acid rain continue the process. Tiny bits of rock typically amount to about half the volume of your soil.

Second, soil contains organic matter, which consists of the by-products and decomposed bodies of plants and animals. Dead leaves, cow manure, earthworm castings, or bacteria that have bitten the dust—all these count as organic matter. Good soil has 5 percent or more organic matter, while the average lawn's soil might have just 1 percent or less, particularly if you bag the grass clippings.

Lastly, topsoil has spaces that hold air and water. These spaces account for nearly half the volume of good soil. Air spaces are important because they allow oxygen and water to reach the roots of plants. Plants absorb water, nutrients, and oxygen through their root hairs.

On a map Vermont and New Hampshire may look like sisters separated by a thin blue line, the Connecticut River. In reality their soils are quite different. Vermont, with the Green Mountains running up its middle like a spine, was created when a huge landmass—including what is now New Hampshire—crashed into it millions of years ago. According to soil scientist Dr. Wendy Sue Harper, formerly of the University of Vermont, Vermont was once part of the continental shelf, the undersea bottom of a shallow sea. When the continents collided, Vermont was pushed into place, the Green Mountains popped up, and bedrock throughout the state was bent and folded.

The type of soil you have depends to a large degree on the type of bedrock that was broken down by erosion and weathering. Limestone bedrock, formed under warm seas in prehistoric times, is common in the Champlain Valley and has produced soils that are richer and less acidic than soils found in the Green Mountains or in Maine or New Hampshire. Those limestone-based soils are some of the best in Vermont for growing a wide variety of plants.

The other major influence on Vermont soils was the action of the glaciers that scoured the earth's surface, grinding up rocks and moving them about. The glaciers were more than 5,000 feet deep—so thick that there is even glacial soil on the tops of the Green Mountains. The glaciers were dirty, pushing up soil and grinding rocks into sand and gravel that became incorporated into the ice. As the glaciers melted, they left deposits—just as the dirty winter snow left by snowplows melts and leaves debris on your lawn in the spring. During glacial times Vermont had two large lakes: Lake Champlain and Lake Hitchcock. The latter drained when the glaciers receded and became the Connecticut River Valley. The bottoms of both lakes accumulated deposits of good soil, which today may be up to 40 feet thick in the Champlain Valley.

According to Wendy Sue Harper, Vermont has about a dozen types of soil that are categorized and named by scientists. Soil deposits are not distributed in broad bands, however, and your neighbor half a mile away may have soil that resembles yours about as much as peonies are like carrots.

If you live near a river or in a floodplain, your soil is probably alluvial soil and pretty good for growing things. Silts, excellent for gardening, were deposited under ancient lakes, particularly along the Connecticut River Valley. Clay is found in the Champlain Valley in areas that were once an inland sea, which allowed fine particles of clay to be deposited over a long period of time. But most of the state is glacial till—fine sandy loam or loam, but with lots of rocks. Areas that are mostly sand and gravel occur where glacial dams broke, leaving outwash deposits. According to a U.S. Department of Agriculture analysis, only 20 percent of Vermont is considered prime farmland.

Types of Soils

There are three basic soil types: sandy, silt, and clay. These three types of soil are mixed in different percentages throughout the state, creating many unique soil profiles.

Sandy soil is made of large mineral particles. Sandy soil lets water pass through quickly, draining off and going down to the subsoil, leaving plants gasping for water on hot, dry summer days. Minerals in a grain of sand are not available to plants. The grains need to be broken down—first physically, then dissolved with the help of acids in the soil—before their nutrients can be taken up by plant root hairs.

Silty soils have medium-size particles; silt holds water well but doesn't tend to stay waterlogged the way clay does. It is a major component of loam.

Clay soils, in contrast, are made of extremely fine mineral particles, each of which can be surrounded by water molecules. They hold water, and are often rich in minerals that plants need and in forms that plants can use. Clay soils, also known as heavy soils, tend to stay wet, and some plants (such as fruit trees) don't do well when their roots are always wet. Clay is easily compacted and when it dries out, it can turn rock hard—making it difficult for gardeners to work in or for plant roots to penetrate.

Loam soil is a well-balanced mixture of sand, silt, clay, and organic matter. Good loam is what we all want but rarely what we have. If you are stuck with soils that aren't perfect, don't despair, soils can be improved—more on that later. **Humus** is another soil component, one that can be of great value to your plants. It is a naturally produced material, a complex breakdown product of organic matter created by microorganisms. It is a key ingredient in all good soils. Its composition varies, depending on the materials it was made from. Humus acts as a kind of piggy bank for plants, because water and mineral elements can attach

Buying Loam

Loam varies considerably in quality. If you intend to buy a few truckloads of it, I recommend checking it out first. After it has been dumped in your yard it is too late to complain. Bring a jug of water and try some of the tests mentioned in the "Getting a Feel for Your Soil" sidebar. If the "loam" is too sticky, it has too much clay in it, and that's not what you want. Remember, soils with good levels of organic matter are darker than average soils; because wet soils are darker than dry ones, check the loam on a dry day—that way you won't be misled.

Getting a Feel for Your Soil

Here are three tests you can perform to learn more about your soil.

1. Pick up a sample of your soil after a rainstorm when your soil is still moist, then rub the sample between your thumb and forefinger. What you are trying to do is determine the size of the particles. Sandy soil will have sharp grains that you can feel and see. Moist clay, however, is smooth and sticky when rubbed between your fingers. Silt is fairly smooth, but not sticky, and contains small grains you can feel. Most soils contain some of each of those three components.

2. Another way to judge your soil is to take a handful of soil and squeeze it into a cylinder. Open your hand. If the soil falls apart when you touch it lightly, you have a sandy soil. If it holds the impression of your hand like modeling clay and can be rolled into long cylinders between your hands, it is dominated by clay. Silt, like Goldilock's bed, is just right: neither too sticky nor too sandy. The longer the cylinder of wet soil you can roll out, the more clay present.

3. This test will give you a rough guide to the composition of your soil: Fill a widemouthed quart jar halfway with soil, add water until nearly full, shake it, and wait. Sand will fall to the bottom almost immediately. Silt (and some organic matter) will generally form a second layer within an hour or two. Some organic matter may float to the surface, depending on its moisture content. Clay will stay suspended in water for a day or two, keeping the water murky and dark. Once the water is clear, you should be able to see three layers and thus approximate the percentage of each in your soil.

If the three layers are all the same color, try draining the water, then use a spoon to sample the layers and feel their texture. Or try the test in a wide plastic container that will allow you to get your fingers on the sediments.

themselves to electrically charged sites on humus particles. Water and minerals are released as needed by plants.

A good topsoil is usually dark in color due to the presence of humus. If you go into the woods and look at the soil, it is usually dark from the decomposition of leaves over the years—and the humus that has been created there.

Other terms used to describe soil are *texture* and *tilth*. Texture refers to the particular blend of soil you have—the mixture of sand, silt, or clay—and how the particles are arranged. If you have lots of organic matter in the soil, and a nice mix of sand, silt, and clay, you should have good texture. Earthworms are great for creating good texture, as they exude compounds—gums and waxes—that hold bits of soil together. Humus is also excellent for improving soil texture.

Tilth is a term that describes how well a soil holds water and allows air to pass through it. Tilth is determined in part by the soil structure. "Good tilth" describes a soil that is light and fluffy. You should be able to poke a screwdriver into the soil with little effort. If the screwdriver does not penetrate easily, your tilth is poor.

Be forewarned that tilth can be ruined by overeager gardeners. Spring in Vermont is usually long and wet, and you may get impatient to start gardening. But if you walk in wet flower beds or try to rototill the vegetable garden before the soil dries out, you can ruin its tilth. Test your soil with the squeeze test described in the "Getting a Feel for Your Soil" sidebar. Unless you can fragment the ball of soil with the tap of a finger, stay out of the garden.

Plants That Tell You about Your Soil

Soil scientist Wendy Sue Harper keeps a list of plants that are indicators for general soil conditions in Vermont when found together in communities. The entire list is too extensive to include here, but I have included some examples that may help you recognize the type of soil conditions in your neighborhood. Remember that there are exceptions to every rule!

Forest canopy plants

- Rich conditions: sugar maple, white ash, basswood, hophornbeam

- Acid or nutrient-poor conditions: paper birch, red maple, mountain laurel

- Disturbed areas: poplars (aspen), pin cherry

- Wet conditions: black spruce, red maple, northern white cedar, tamarack

- Dry conditions or shallow soil: red oak, white oak, eastern red cedar

Understory plants

- Rich conditions: bloodroot, Dutchman's breeches, herb robert, wild leeks

- Acid or nutrient-poor conditions: blueberry, cranberry, Labrador tea, pink lady's slipper, sheep laurel

- Disturbed areas: bush honeysuckle, buckthorn, barberry, burdock

- Wet conditions: winterberry, blueberry, cattails, marsh marigolds

- Dry conditions or shallow soil: wild columbine, woodland sedge, little bluestem

To Understand *Your* Soil, Get It Tested

A soil test done on your soil will tell you the specifics of your soil: its pH (how acidic or alkaline it is), how much organic matter is in the soil, and what levels of important soil minerals are present.

Before you start your first garden, and every three or four years thereafter, it's a good idea to have your soil tested. University of Vermont Extension offers this service for $14. If you are growing vegetables, don't be a cheapskate! Pay the extra $10 at least once to see if there is lead, cadmium, or other heavy metals in the soil. Heavy metals can be harmful if taken up by plants that are consumed by people, especially pregnant women and small children. You can download the soil test form and instructions, just Google "UVM soil tests." Or you can call UVM Extension—see chapter 14 for details. Plan ahead: In spring you may have to wait for weeks to get your test results back from the lab.

When should you test your soil? Although any time of year is fine, fall is best. A soil test will give you recommendations for improving your soil, and improvements take time. If you need to sweeten your soil, for example, applying the limestone in fall lets the limestone dissolve and disperse in your soil ahead of spring planting.

Drainage

Plants have preferences just like you do. Some prefer dry soils, others thrive in wet ones, while most garden plants do best in soil that stays slightly moist but drains well after a rainstorm. Drainage depends on several things: soil type, soil texture, subsoil, and hilliness.

You can learn much about your soil by digging a hole 24 inches wide and deep. Try to keep the sides of the hole smooth and straight so that you can see the color of the soil. The topsoil, if it is rich in organic matter, should be a dark brown, and it might be just a couple of inches deep or, if you're lucky, more. Next, you might have a layer of clay or sand or stones that may be reddish orange to brown in color. Farther down, near the bottom of the hole, look for gray-colored soil. That discoloration indicates the water table, the level where soil stays saturated with water for much of the year. In the spring you may reach water before your hole is 2 feet deep.

You may hit bedrock or a layer of ledge before you dig 2 feet down, too. If your property is flat, or nearly flat, and you are on bedrock, your soil will not drain well—and that will affect what kinds of flowers and trees will do well for you. Big trees may blow over in high winds if roots can't go down to an adequate depth. Nut trees, in particular, send taproots down deep into the soil, and they are not a good choice for shallow soils.

Here's a simple test to learn about your soil's drainage: Dig a hole 2 feet in diameter and 8 inches deep with sloping sides. Run water from the hose into the hole until it is full. Time how long it takes to drain. Sandy soils drain almost immediately. Heavy clay might take all day or longer. If it drains in an hour or two, you are in good shape. This test is not precise—it is affected by how much rain you have had in recent days: The wetter the soil, the longer it will take to drain off. But the test will give you a rough idea of the drainage conditions your plants face.

Soil pH and Plant Nutrients

The soil pH test measures the acidity or alkalinity of your garden soil and rates it on a scale of 1 to 14, with 7 being neutral. The scale is logarithmic, meaning that a pH of 6 is ten times sweeter than one with a pH of 5, and a hundred times sweeter than one with a pH of 4. Different plants may need different pHs. Most plants do well in the range of 6 to 7, which is slightly acidic to neutral. If you have very acidic soil, say in the 4.5 to 5.5 range, most authorities would tell you to add ground limestone or wood ashes to sweeten the soil, bringing it closer to neutral.

What's the big deal about soil pH? If the pH of your soil is too acidic (with a pH of 5.5 or less), the minerals calcium, phosphorus, and magnesium may be present in the soil but tied up and unavailable to plants. It's like being given a can of tuna for dinner but no can opener to open it. Soils too sweet (with too high a pH, perhaps caused by the annual application of ashes without first testing the soil) may tie up phosphorus, iron, copper, zinc, boron, and manganese. When the soil pH is wrong, a plant may languish, turn yellow, or show other signs of nutrient deficiencies, even though the nutrients are in the soil. The plant just can't access them.

Be aware that acidic soil can also be a sign of a soil that has few minerals left to offer your plants. It works like this: Plants give off hydrogen ions from their root tips, trading the hydrogen ions for minerals in the soil—notably potassium, calcium, magnesium, iron, copper, zinc, and nickel. A pH test is actually a measure of hydrogen ions. If all the minerals just mentioned have been used up, there will be lots of hydrogen ions in the soil, and the test will indicate that it's highly acidic. Just adding limestone to the soil will not solve the problem. Yes, the pH will be better, but if the soil is depleted of minerals, your plants will still suffer. Adding organic matter and a bagged organic fertilizer will help replenish the soil with needed minerals. Your soil test will tell you what minerals need to be added.

Chemical Elements That Plants Need

We've just touched on a number of chemical elements that plants need but can't use if the pH is wrong. In fact, scientists have determined that plants require a total of sixteen or seventeen different chemical elements to live and thrive. Most of these chemical elements are found as compounds (generally as salts in chemical fertilizers) that chemically join two elements, such as potassium and chloride. These compounds need to be broken down into two parts known as ions, which carry electrical charges, to be used by plants. The breakdown process can be aided by water and by the actions of microorganisms in a healthy soil.

Macronutrients

Let's first look at some of the more important elements—known as macronutrients—and how plants use them:

Carbon: Plants get their carbon from carbon dioxide, which is present in the air. They absorb it through stomata, or little holes on the underside of leaves. During the day, plants combine carbon dioxide and water through the process of photosynthesis to create sugars and carbohydrates that fuel all life processes in plants—and ultimately in animals.

Oxygen: Although oxygen is needed by plants for metabolic functions, plants are not as dependent on oxygen as animals are. Plants get oxygen through their roots, not through their leaves. A waterlogged soil, however, can eventually drown a plant because it deprives the plant of oxygen.

Hydrogen: Like carbon and oxygen, hydrogen is an integral part of plant structures.

Carbon, oxygen, and hydrogen can be considered "free" nutrients—gardeners don't need to provide them. The next three macronutrients, known as "the big three," are often added to soils by gardeners.

Nitrogen: Plants generally absorb nitrogen from the soil in the form of ammonium or nitrate ions. Nitrogen is used by plants to make complex chemicals that we call proteins. Gardeners add nitrogen-containing fertilizers to stimulate green growth and to make plants get big fast, but too much nitrogen can keep plants from flowering or producing fruit, and high quantities can "burn" roots or even kill plants.

Phosphorus: This element comes in a variety of forms—naturally occurring forms derived from rocks, and other forms produced in chemical factories. Phosphorus is important for "roots and fruits"—developing good root systems and for promoting blooming, seed production, and fruits.

Potassium is important for developing strong cell walls, which plants need to resist environmental stresses like drought and extremes of temperature, either hot or cold. Potassium is also involved in carbohydrate metabolism and cell division.

Three other elements are considered secondary macronutrients—necessary for plant health, but not in the same quantities as the big three.

Calcium is an important element in cell metabolism. It helps plants build proteins and take up nitrogen. It is a key element in developing strong cell membranes. Tomatoes, peppers, and squashes grown in low-calcium soils may develop blossom-end rot.

Magnesium is a part of the chlorophyll molecules needed for photosynthesis and is involved with enzyme use.

Sulfur is necessary for making proteins and fats. Most soils have sulfur, and it is also found in our acid rain. Sulfur makes onions pungent.

Micronutrients

Plants also need the following elements—called micronutrients—but in smaller amounts than the elements above. Be aware that not all fertilizers contain micronutrients. A natural, organic fertilizer will provide micronutrients, but a conventional chemical fertilizer will not.

Iron is needed for making chlorophyll, enzymes, and proteins. An iron deficiency in rhododendrons can cause a yellowing of leaves known as interveinal chlorosis. Iron can be unavailable to plants if the soil is too acidic.

Chlorine is needed in photosynthesis and cell metabolism.

Manganese is also involved in making chlorophyll and is needed for making some vitamins. Peas are sensitive to low levels of manganese.

Zinc: Although not much zinc is needed, a little is required for building proteins and plant growth hormones, especially in corn and peaches.

Copper and **boron:** Needed in even smaller quantities, these elements are important for various plant metabolic functions.

Molybdenum: Only a miniscule amount—two parts per million—of this metal is needed, but it is essential for protein synthesis and for the bacteria involved in nitrogen fixation.

Nickel: Small amounts are needed for plant metabolism.

How to Improve Your Soil

Okay, you have the results of your soil test in hand and it reveals a nutrient deficiency. What do you add to improve your soil?

First remember that Mother Nature knows best. Repeat that as needed, and as loudly as needed, especially if your spouse tries to convince you that all can be fixed with a good dose of chemical fertilizer. Compost and organic fertilizers provide all the nutrients and micronutrients needed by plants.

Chemical fertilizers—and by that I mean fertilizers created in factories using petroleum products and harsh chemical reactions—are used to provide three useful elements: nitrogen, phosphorus, and potassium. Chemical fertilizers will not adjust the pH, add organic matter, or encourage beneficial microorganisms to live in your soil. In fact, some experiments have shown that chemical fertilizers can even make beneficial bacteria go dormant. Chemical fertilizers will not improve drainage or water retention, either, but there is something that will: adding compost and organic amendments. Let's look at what's available.

The Magic of Compost: Compost Helps Soil Structure

Adding compost improves soil structure and a soil's ability to hold moisture and drain well. Imagine a wire basket full of golf balls. Turn the hose on it and the water pours right through. That's how a sandy soil works. Now add lots of tiny little sponges (representing bits of compost), each smaller than a golf ball, and stir in. Turn on the hose. The wire basket still drains quickly, but it holds some water, just as sand will if you add compost.

Next imagine a bowl of dry baking flour. Add water, and it puddles on the top. That's like a clay soil. If you add enough water and stir, you have a sticky mess. If it dries out, it's hard as a rock. Now imagine mixing in wheat germ, representing compost. Wheat germ has bigger particles than flour and helps to improve its texture. The resulting mixture is much easier to work with than straight flour.

Not only does compost improve soil structure, it also provides the full range of nutrients. True, compost is not high in nitrogen, the element that drives fast green growth. But a good compost has everything that a plant needs, and more. Compost feeds the micro-organisms that work with plants, the bacteria and fungi that process raw materials and convert them into forms usable by plants. It is a slow, natural process.

Adding Fertility with Organic Fertilizers

Soil tests rarely give recommendations for increasing nitrogen, as nitrogen levels change rapidly from day to day and week to week, depending on temperature, moisture levels, and other factors. If you have poor soil that is low in organic matter, or if your soil tests show low levels of phosphorus and potassium, you probably need to boost nitrogen levels, too. This can be done with the application of bagged organic fertilizer. Organic fertilizers are made from plant

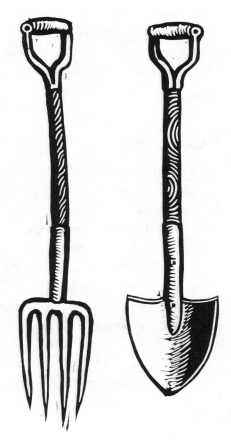

and animal products such as seaweed, ground seashells, blood meal, and peanut hulls. Naturally occurring mineral products like rock phosphate and greensand are also present in them. These fertilizers provide the full range of elements needed by plants.

I have very high levels of organic matter in my vegetable garden, but I add a little bagged organic fertilizer at planting time with most transplants, stirring in a small handful of Pro-Gro (my organic fertilizer of choice) into a hole 12 inches or more across. This fertilizer provides extra nitrogen that gives my plants a boost when starting out. I don't add fertilizer to the soil for peppers or annual flowers—they don't need it. In midsummer I scratch some in next to my carrots to increase their size. And I add some each time I plant a perennial, as I know it adds lots of micronutrients in addition to the "big three."

Organic fertilizers depend on microorganisms to convert them into forms that can be used by plants. Unlike chemical fertilizers, a big rainstorm won't dissolve your organic fertilizers, so they won't end up in our water systems. They are broken down into usable forms more quickly in hot weather—when they are needed most.

Applying Other Soil Amendments

Animal manures contain nitrogen and other useful nutrients but can introduce weed seeds. Cow and horse manures should always be composted before using. Sheep, llama, goat, and rabbit manures are generally not weedy and are good amendments. Chicken manure is so high in nitrogen it can burn roots, so compost it, too.

Ground limestone provides calcium and helps to neutralize acids in the soil. If the soil is too acidic, some minerals will be tied up and may not be readily available to your plants. If you buy dolomitic limestone, you also get magnesium, another element used by plants. If your soil is very acidic, say at the pH 4.5 to 5.0 range, you shouldn't try to bring the pH up to the optimal 6.0 to 6.8 range in one year. Three years, with testing each year, would be better.

The UVM Extension will suggest how much limestone to add when you get the results of your soil test. You might want to get an inexpensive pH test kit at your local garden center and test yearly until your soil approaches neutral. There are several forms of limestone: pelletized, ground, and hydrated or slaked. The latter two are not for gardeners, but any limestone you buy at a garden center should be fine.

Wood ashes: Like limestone, wood ashes sweeten the

> ## Don't Turn Your Garden into Concrete!
>
> If you have a heavy clay soil, don't add sand, thinking that will solve the problem—you may end up with something like concrete. A clay-and-sand mixture can turn hard as a rock when it dries out. Instead, add in *lots* of compost.

soil, making soil less acidic. Ashes may be free from your wood-stove, but don't just mindlessly add them every year. Test pH yearly before adding them to the garden. Soil scientist Wendy Sue Harper says wood ashes are roughly equivalent to limestone when calculating how much to use. Ash is very fine, and you should be careful not to inhale it—apply it on a day with no wind, and wear a mask. No particulate matter is good for your lungs. Wood ashes act faster than limestone because the texture is so fine. They also are a good source of potassium.

Rock phosphate, black rock phosphate, colloidal phosphate: These are all good forms of phosphorus for organic gardeners. They are derived from rocks and release phosphorus to plants slowly, over a multiyear period—up to five or seven years. Rock phosphate is the slowest to be taken up by plants, colloidal phosphate the fastest. Rock phosphate also contains 33 percent calcium and has about 20 percent of the neutralizing effect of limestone. Colloidal phosphate is the best choice for sandy soil as it also contains clay, which can help to bind sand particles and increase its ability to hold on to nutrients and water.

What Do Those Numbers on a Bag of Fertilizer Mean?

They list the contents of the bag as percentages of total weight. The first number is always nitrogen, the second phosphate, the last potash, a potassium compound. Thus 5-10-5 contains 5 percent nitrogen usable to plants by weight, 10 percent phosphorus, and 5 percent potassium. Chemical fertilizers contain filler to help keep gardeners from burning the roots of their plants and to make the fertilizer easier to spread. Organic fertilizers are made from plant and animal by-products and are approved by an agency to certify that they are good for organic growers.

Organic Fertilizers Available in Vermont

These organic fertilizers, and perhaps others, are available throughout the state. Look for the word "organic" on the bag. Some others will say "all natural," which is good, but not the best.

Pro-Gro: Made in Bradford from seaweed, fishmeal, ground oyster shells, rock phosphate, whey, blood meal, compost, and agricultural by-products like peanut meal. It is my fertilizer of choice. It's a 5-3-4 fertilizer, with about one-third of the nitrogen immediately available and the rest released slowly, as are most of the other ingredients. The website norganics.com has many excellent technical reports for advanced gardeners.

Blue Seal: Their Safe 'N Simple Plant Food is a 5-5-5 made from soy, alfalfa, and fish meals. It is readily available around the state wherever Blue Seal feeds are sold.

Espoma: This company makes a variety of fertilizers from organic ingredients. Plant-Tone, the all-purpose fertilizer, is a 5-3-3. Espoma fertilizer bags, unlike those of most other brands, list guaranteed content of many of the micronutrients needed by plants.

Phosphate attaches to soil particles on contact and thus does not migrate through the soil like nitrogen fertilizers—unless abnormally high levels of phosphate are present. When planting trees or shrubs, I do not use nitrogen-containing fertilizers, but I am always sure to add rock phosphate in the hole to get it down deep where it will be used. Manure from dairy barns may be very high in phosphate and can be detrimental if washed into streams. Use it moderately, and get your soil tested if you use a lot of fresh manure.

Greensand: This is another good natural additive to soil. It is primarily sold as an additive to provide potassium, but it also contains magnesium, iron, calcium, phosphorus, and some thirty different micronutrients. It comes from an ancient undersea deposit in New Jersey. The primary ingredient is a mineral known as glauconite, an iron potassium silicate compound.

Rock dust or rock flour: I've been adding finely ground rock powders to my soils for the past fifteen years or more. I get it from places that cut granite for tombstones. Rock dust is sold commercially in bags as Azomite, which contains "minerals from A to Z" according to the ads. Not often found in garden centers, Azomite may be purchased from seed companies like Fedco of Maine (see chapter 14). Garden centers that sell Pro-Gro can order Azomite from the maker of Pro-Gro. Just ask.

Fine rock powders seem to energize plants, getting them to start off faster. I've particularly observed this with my potatoes. Applied late in the season, it has appeared to help in the production of my sweet peppers. My observations are anecdotal, not scientific, however. Years of controlled tests are needed.

When I interviewed retired professor Ward Chesworth of the University of Guelph in Ontario, he postulated that the fine rock powders may provide some of the trace elements that the glaciers would provide—the next time they return. I liked his metaphor that farmers "have been making tea with the same bag for 10,000 years." Granite dust may supply minerals that scientists have yet to identify as important.

How much rock dust to use? The literature says you can use fourteen pounds per 100 square feet, but some other gardeners use three times that amount. I just sprinkle some on at planting time. I'm intrigued by the stuff, in part due to an article I read about the farmers in the Hunza Valley of Pakistan who irrigate their crops with "glacial milk"—water from a glacier that is high in fine rock particles. They routinely live to be over one hundred years old, and there are those who attribute the Hunza farmers' longevity to the minerals in their food. Of course, their lifestyle and diet is much different than ours, too. Go to remineralize.org for more information.

Planting Green Manures and Cover Crops

Cover crops (also called green manures) are grown to improve the soil, not for food. Cover crops such as buckwheat, clover, and annual rye can produce lots of organic matter than can be incorporated into the soil where it will break down, feeding the bacteria, fungi, and earthworms that help your plants to grow. If you have sandy soil or a heavy clay soil, or any soil that is low in organic matter, you may wish to consider growing a cover crop.

Farmers often plant cover crops to hold on to soil nutrients that might wash away over the winter by planting them in September. Annual rye will grow until cold weather sets in, and then die. In the spring the organic matter is tilled into the soil, along with the nutrients the rye took from the soil in the fall. Winter rye will survive our winters, and start growing again in the early spring.

Buckwheat can be planted in the spring and allowed to grow just 6 to 8 inches tall, then mowed down and turned into the soil. That provides a quick shot of nutrition for soil microbes. But if you don't cut it down, it will blossom and set seeds that will fall into the soil and compete with your veggies just like weeds.

Most gardeners who use cover crops use rototillers to work in the stems and stalks because it is much easier than doing it by hand with a fork. One note of warning: If you plant rye, know that it releases chemicals into the soil that inhibit other plants from growing. So you must wait two to three weeks after mixing it into the soil before trying to grow something else.

Final Thoughts

What's the key to success in the garden? Good soil. Add organic matter and good compost. Get a soil test done. Stay away from chemical fertilizers; they never provide the full range of minerals needed by plants nor do they improve soil texture or structure. And lastly, be patient. It takes years to get your soil to the quality you'd like to have. But you will get there—if you keep at it.

Growing Seasons

From the cold Northeast Kingdom to the relative warmth of Burlington and Brattleboro, the climate of Vermont varies considerably. Gardeners in the Green Mountains must plant with a slightly different palette of plants than those along the Connecticut River, but all Vermonters share similar challenges. Throughout the state most perennial flowers, trees, and shrubs only start to wake up and grow in April after their long winter's nap. Annual flowers and vegetables aren't able to survive and thrive in most parts of Vermont until the weather warms up in late May, or even mid-June in the colder places. Even frost-hardy veggies like peas don't grow much until the soil warms up and the sun has strength. However, there is much a gardener can do to stretch the growing season and to keep tender plants happy despite the cold.

Determining Your Hardiness Zone

Vermont spans three USDA Hardiness Zones: 3, 4, and 5. The best way to decide what zone you live in is to keep track of the coldest temperatures each winter at your particular site—or talk with a neighbor who has done so. Keep in mind that temperatures vary from year to year, so you can't buy trees or perennials just based on what last winter was like.

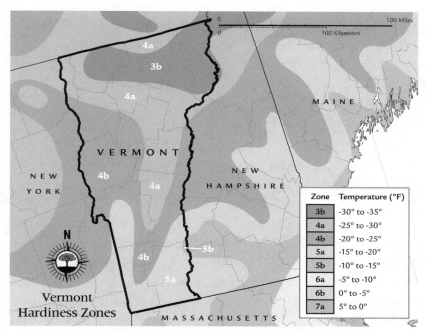

The 1990 USDA Hardiness Zone map shows the average coldest temperatures in Vermont. Take these zone ranges with a grain of salt. Due to the presence of microclimates, zones can vary tremendously, even within a town.

Hardiness zones are important considerations when buying perennial flowers, shrubs, and trees: They limit what you can grow. Even a few days at minus 30 degrees may kill your favorite rose. If you're new in town, ask a neighbor how cold it gets, or talk to the folks at your local family-run gardening center—they know what survives here.

Most of the state is in Zone 4, which means that on an average winter—and we all know there is no such thing—the temperature in your garden will go down to at least minus 20, but no colder than minus 30. Near the Canadian border and in the Green Mountains, temperatures can get even colder: The average coldest temperatures are 30 to 40 degrees below zero, qualifying as Zone 3, even though these extreme temperatures may occur only for a few days each year—or every few years. Along Lake Champlain and in the southern parts of the state, gardeners only have to endure 10 to 20 degrees below zero, which is considered Zone 5.

Weather Records for Vermont

The two key dates for vegetable gardeners are the last frost in the spring and the first frost in the fall. But where do you get this information?

The state does not have any easy way for the gardeners to access weather records for recent years. The county soil surveys prepared by the USDA do include weather information, but it is a bit outdated. The Windham County soil survey, for example, has data from 1951 to 1980, which is interesting but not necessarily relevant given recent climatic changes. According to the Windham County soil survey, one year in ten the last spring frost is later than May 28, and five years in ten it is later than May 14. The records show that one year in ten the first autumn frost is earlier than October 11, and five years in ten it is earlier than October 27. But those data were recorded in Bellows Falls, and we all know that temperatures in the countryside tend to be colder than in town or along a river or lake.

The World Wide Web offers information about weather and climate, but website addresses seem to change often. Probably the best idea is just to use your search engine to report on the "last frost date in Vermont." Coldest temperatures in your area can be helpful, too, especially when selecting trees and perennials.

The important information to know is your first and last frost dates. Each garden plot is different, so averages don't help much. I wait to plant frost-sensitive plants in the garden until any chance of frost has passed. In my Zone 4 garden, the last spring frost is usually in late May, but I wait until June 5 or later to plant things that might be killed or injured by frost. That allows the ground to warm up more, too.

Some gardeners—including me—try to stretch the growing season in the fall; we cover tender plants with old sheets and blankets or spread huge pieces of plastic over our pumpkin patches. We know that an early frost can be followed by six weeks of warm, even hot weather. Other gardeners fold their cards early and let Jack Frost (or Jill Frost, if you prefer) finish off the garden.

Microclimates

Even on your own land the temperature and growing conditions can vary considerably. My vegetable garden often gets frost when the flower beds around the house do not. That's because the house is 15 feet higher in elevation and the house acts as a reservoir of warmth, radiating heat at night.

Cold air is denser than warm air—the reverse of the principle used to fly hot-air balloons—so it tends to flow downhill. Valleys often get frosts when the hilltops are spared them.

Exposed rock, particularly if dark in color, will absorb heat in the day and radiate it at night. I sometimes place black stones around the base of heat-loving plants like eggplants or peppers to help them stay warmer at night.

The top of a hillside, though in full sun, may not be the best place for a garden if it is constantly windy; the wind will cool and dry the plants all summer long. A barn, a hedge, or a wooded area may spill some shade onto your plants yet encourage them to grow better by blocking the wind.

In Vermont the best exposure for warmth-loving plants is on a gentle hillside facing the southeast. The spring sun will warm it first, and a slope helps to drain away excess moisture, an important factor in getting soils ready to plant. North-facing slopes are poor choices for growing much of anything but hay or forest.

Sun and Shade

This far north the sun changes its arc considerably as seasons change. Before you plant an orchard or create an extensive flower bed, you should keep records of the patterns of sun and shade over the course of a year. The number of hours of direct sun is important to your plants, and a row of evergreens will shade your plot differently in April than it will in July.

Full sun is most important in spring, to warm the soil, and in midsummer when your plants do the bulk of their growing. It doesn't matter so much if the house shades a flower bed in early spring or late fall—your plants are less active then anyway.

Extending Your Growing Seasons

There are many ways to extend the Vermont growing seasons, including such things as warming the soil, choosing plant varieties that do well in cold climates, and even building simple hoop houses or cold frames to protect plants. Let's look at your options more closely.

Get an Early Start

Impatient to get going in the spring? One of the best ways to get an early start is to prepare your vegetable beds in the fall. That way you can sneak in a few seeds or frost-hardy plants without ruining soil structure by working in wet soil in spring.

In the fall, clean up the vegetable garden of that year's weeds and dead plants. Add compost to the beds and work it in. Then hill up the soil in beds 30 inches wide with walkways in between. No need to use planks to contain the soil, just mound it up about 6 inches above the paths and work in some compost. These raised beds will warm up more easily and drain faster than flat soil.

Even if the air temperatures are warm in the spring, wet soils don't warm up quickly. And you need both: warm days and warm soil. Most plants prefer soil temperatures to reach 60 degrees before being planted.

On a sunny day in spring, you can heat up the soil by stretching clear plastic sheeting over your beds. Pin it down with agricultural staples, rocks, planks, or soil so that it won't blow away or let cool air in. Clear plastic heats the soil better than black plastic because the sun goes right through it and directly warms your soil. Black plastic will eventually warm the soil, however, and it is used by some gardeners to keep weeds from germinating.

I've measured temperatures above 100 under clear plastic on a sunny day when the air temperature was only 65 degrees. This method, called solarization, will also cook any annual weed seeds that have already germinated. A few days of solarizing the soil doesn't raise the temperature much, but it helps. I've never kept clear plastic down for more than a week. Be prepared to experiment. Try not to disturb the soil when planting seeds in the warmed soil, as soil deeper down will still be plenty chilly.

When Can I Start My Vegetable Garden?

It might be exciting to get outside and plant things in mid-April, and some Vermont gardeners do, but there's not much point to planting early if your soil is wet and cold. Early crops that grow in cold weather include spinach, peas, and hardy lettuces. But if you plant too early, seeds can rot—and nothing grows very much when the soil is 40 degrees or cooler. Early to mid-May is a safe planting date for those cold-weather crops most years. Ask an old-timer in your town for advice.

Remember: Don't rototill the soil or walk on areas you will be planting when the soil is wet, or you may damage the soil structure and tilth of your garden.

A new type of plastic sheeting was developed at the University of New Hampshire by Professor Brent Loy. Called IRT mulch, it allows heat-producing infrared rays to pass through and reach the ground but keeps out visible light, thus suppressing weeds. It's available from Fedco Seeds or Johnny's Selected Seeds (see the resources in chapter 14).

Keep Going in Fall

You can extend the growing season in the fall, too. I refuse to let my basil, cucumbers, and squash plants get turned black and mushy by a September frost. I know that there will be plenty of warm weather still ahead, so I go out and cover them every clear night when frost is predicted or when the temperature is less than 50

Will Your Veggies and Flowers Survive a Light Frost?

No: Basil, beans, cilantro, cukes, dill, eggplants, melons, peppers, pumpkins, all kinds of squash, and tomatoes. All annual flowers are frost sensitive, but some will survive light frosts.

Yes: Artichokes, arugula, broccoli, cabbage, carrots, cauliflower, celery, chives, corn, garlic, greens, horseradish, kale, kohlrabi, leeks, lettuce, onions, oregano, parsley, parsnips, peas, radishes, spinach, swiss chard, thyme, and turnips. Perennial flowers are generally not frost sensitive, and some spring bulbs like snowdrops will push up flower stalks through frozen soil and survive repeated nights of temperatures in the twenties.

Potato vines will get killed by frost, but the spuds won't get hurt. Rosemary is a perennial in Mediterranean climates and will survive light frosts, but it needs to come inside to winter over.

degrees at 5:00 p.m. I use old bedspreads, sheets, plastic sheeting, and blue tarps. I use rocks and bricks to keep the covers in place, particularly if it's windy. I like to get the covers in place by 5:00 p.m. or earlier, before the air gets too cold, so that the covers hold in the daytime heat soaked up by the earth before that heat dissipates.

There are times when I forget to cover, or when the clouds—which serve as a kind of giant blanket—move off after I've gone to bed, and I wake up to frost on the garden. All is not lost: I take the hose and wash off the frost, which, for many vegetables, may give them a reprieve. That, of course, depends on how cold it got. A frost of 31 degrees is survivable for many things, but a frost of 26 degrees is not.

How long can you extend the gardening season? You can make it as long as you want it to be, within reason. If you start spinach on May 1 and still have carrots and Brussels sprouts in the ground on Thanksgiving Day, as we often do, your growing season is about 200 days. But for cold-sensitive crops like tomatoes and pumpkins, the best you can do in Vermont is more like 100 to 120 days—and sometimes less than that.

Pick the Right Varieties

Select varieties of vegetables and flowers that are said to do well in cold climates.

Then, to maximize your crops, select at least some varieties with the shortest number of days possible to harvest. An heirloom 'Brandywine' tomato can take eighty-five days from seedling to sandwich, while 'Early Girl' (a patio-type tomato) requires only sixty days; my favorite cherry tomato, 'Sun Gold', takes only fifty-seven days—four weeks earlier than Brandywines! I plant several varieties each year so that I get an early crop, a batch of heirlooms with their extra sweet flavor, and a crop of the bigger tomatoes that generally take longer to mature. This way if an early frost catches me unprepared and I lose my plants, the year is not lost for tomatoes.

Some seed catalogs or packets don't tell all they should. For starters, they *assume* that gardeners will know that a tomato labeled "sixty-five days to harvest" means *sixty-five days from transplant*. They *assume* you know that vegetables that are never started indoors (like carrots or beets, for example) are labeled with the number of days from planting seeds *outdoors* to harvest. Read the fine print so you won't be disappointed by planting tomato, pepper, or eggplant seeds outdoors. In Vermont they won't succeed that way.

Learning from an Old-timer

According to my late friend Lewis Hill of Greensboro, who gardened in Vermont for more than seventy years, the weather is always unpredictable. "It's hard to talk fast enough to discuss it properly because it changes so fast," he told me. The author of seventeen books on gardening, his 1987 classic, *Cold-Climate Gardening: How to Extend Your Growing Season by at Least 30 Days*, is still in print and is a great resource for Vermont gardeners. His old-time humor makes it fun to read, too.

Give Your Early Plants Sweaters

You can protect early plantings from frost by covering them with spun-bonded polypropylene agricultural fabric, also known as row covers. The best known of the products is Reemay, but many types are now available, each differing in weight and ability to let light pass through (70 percent to 90 percent light transmission fabrics are available). Agribon is another reputable brand.

Row covers can be placed right over the soil and pinned down after planting or draped over wire hoops to create tents or tunnels. Unlike clear plastic, this fabric breathes, allowing temperatures to moderate and moisture to pass through. The heaviest of row covers can protect frost-sensitive plants down to 26 degrees. Row covers are also great for protecting your tasty young plants from insect pests like striped cucumber beetles and flea beetles. I keep Reemay over cukes and squashes until they start to blossom, then I remove it—row covers keep the pollinating insects out as well as the pests.

Another type of plant sweater is a product known as a Wall-o-Water, available at most garden centers and in many seed catalogs. This device encloses plants in an 18-by-18-inch plastic cylinder that holds three gallons of water in plastic baffles. During the day the Wall-o-Water absorbs heat, storing it in the water; heat radiates out at night. During cold times the top can be drawn in, creating a toasty tepee. I've used them, and they do work. The maker claims it will protect frost-sensitive plants down to 16 degrees. They are also good for warming the soil if you set them out a week or two before planting. As tomato plants get bigger, the Wall-o-Water can be opened up to let the plants emerge. A Wall-o-Water should last several years.

Hot caps are another way to protect plants in the spring. The cheapest are homemade: Cut the bottom out of gallon milk jugs and place them over new transplants. Take off the jug cap to keep excessive heat from building up during the day, and put the cap

Does the Full Moon Accompany the First Frost?

Folklore says that the last frost of the spring coincides with the full moon. But is that true? My friend Sally Wellborn of Cornish, New Hampshire (who lives 5 miles from Vermont), kept records of frost dates for more than twenty years. When her son, Gwyn Gallagher, was a college student, he decided to test the theory. He took his mother's records and correlated them with the phases of the moon over all those years. He determined that the moon does not affect the temperature.

back on at night. In Victorian times gardeners put glass bell-shaped cloches over their plants to shelter them. But it would be easy to inadvertently cook a tender plant with one of those.

Build a Simple Greenhouse or Hoop House

Owning a simple unheated greenhouse or hoop house is a great way to extend the seasons and to grow heat-loving plants faster than their counterparts living outside in Vermont's often chilly weather. Chilly nights—in the forties, say—are discouraging to things like peppers, so I grow those heat lovers in a hoop house I built myself.

Where to Find Greenhouse Plastic

Regular clear polyethylene might last a year or less on a hoop house, so you need heavier plastic that also resists degradation by ultraviolet light. Suppliers like Growers Supply want to sell big pieces, more than you need. I got a piece free from my local greenhouse—used and dirty, but usable. You might be able to buy a new piece from a commercial grower if the grower buys it by the roll and has some left over.

Commercial greenhouses with aluminum frames glazed with flat panels of 4- or 6-mil polycarbonate "glass" are readily available but a bit pricey for my budget. Growers Supply (see chapter 14) sells many different models, some starting under $1,000. Gardener's Supply in Burlington, Vermont (see chapter 14) sells a variety of them through its catalog, but you can also go to Burlington to look at greenhouses in some seasons—call first to be sure. Gardener's Supply even has one that arrives on a flatbed truck fully assembled, ready to set in place.

If you enjoy building things and are a decent weekend carpenter, you can construct your own hoop house for just a fraction of the price. I built one that

How to Build Your Own Hoop House

I built my on-a-budget hoop house by first selecting a site that was flat and in full sun. I established a straight line with a string and two stakes. Next I took 2-foot-long pieces of ¾-inch metal electrical conduit and drove it 12 inches into the ground every 2 feet along the string. I angled the conduit just ever so slightly out—away from what would become the interior of the hoop house.

Next I used a framing square, tape measure, and an 8-foot 2x4 to establish another line parallel to the first and 8 feet away from it. I set up another string and drove conduit along that line opposite the first row of rebar.

I purchased twelve 10-foot lengths of 1-inch diameter PVC pipe, the kind that electricians use. I glued these together in pairs and let the cement cure for fifteen minutes before proceeding. Then I slipped one end of what was now a 20-foot pipe over a piece of conduit that was sticking out of the ground, and I gently bent the PVC pipe over, creating a hoop. I slipped the other end of the pipe over the conduit opposite it, 8 feet away. I repeated this five times, and the basic structure was in place. It looked like the real thing! (Or the ribcage of a great blue whale.)

I then stabilized the hoops by attaching three 10-foot lengths of wood strapping (1½-by-¾-inch lumber) to the plastic pipe. I did this by screwing right through the wood into the ribs—the plastic pipes—using a portable drill and 1½-inch galvanized Phillips screws. I attached strapping on either side of the hoop house 30 inches above ground and parallel to it, and then I added a piece on top, right down the middle.

The end walls needed to be framed up next: one end for a door, the other for a window that would

continued

allow me to regulate temperatures by opening and closing it. But first I took a hoe and scraped out a trench where the walls would stand. I made it about 8 inches wide by 6 inches deep and filled it with crushed stone, making sure it was level. One should never use pressure-treated wood near food crops, but untreated wood rots quickly if it's in contact with soil and water. The gravel allows the wood to dry out and last longer. You can also paint your 2x4s with linseed oil to prolong their useful life.

I put a 2x4 on top of the gravel from one side of the hoop house to the other and screwed through the pipe on each side with a 3½-inch screw. This served as the base for the wall. Then I framed up a door frame for the screen door I intended to use. I allowed an extra ¾inch on each side to keep the door from jamming if the wood swelled. I attached the uprights to the plastic hoops with plumber's strap. This comes as a roll of flexible metal strap an inch wide that is full of holes for screws. I wrapped straps around the hoop, then screwed the straps to the 2x4s.

At the other end of the hoop house, I framed an opening for an aluminum storm window, the kind with two pieces of glass that slide up and down on tracks. I positioned the window up as high as possible so I could vent heat on hot days.

The next job is a two-person task that should be done on a day with little wind: fitting the plastic sheeting over the hoop house. I used a piece 30 feet long and 25 feet wide, which allowed for plenty of extra on all sides. Two of us pulled it up and over the hoop house. I fixed the plastic in place with three more 10-foot lengths of strapping, sandwiching the plastic between these and the strapping already in place. The storm window went in place easily. I wrapped the

screen door with plastic and added a latch to keep it from blowing open.

The hoop house has been remarkably successful. It has held up to winter winds and snow that didn't always slide off. For extra strength I braced the end walls with 2x4s, each set at a 45-degree angle between the wall and ground inside.

is 10 feet long, 8 feet wide, and tall enough to walk in. It took me about eight hours to build and cost me $100, not counting the materials I had kicking around the barn. Those included an old aluminum storm window, a screen door with a ruined screen, and a big sheet of used greenhouse plastic that I got free. See the sidebar "How to Build Your Own Hoop House" for details about my project.

I start spinach and other early greens each fall in the hoop house. They get established, then go dormant until the ground thaws in March or April. Most of them start growing again (though I lose a few). Later, come summer, I grow peppers inside the hoop house where it is hotter and where I can control the amount of water they get—they don't like wet soil, having originated in Mexico. I also plant a few tomatoes in the hoop house each year, including one heirloom that takes forever outdoors but produces earlier in the hoop house.

Use Hot Boxes and Cold Frames

Gardeners have been cheating Jack Frost each spring for generations with cold frames. My grandfather built wooden boxes for early vegetables, covering them with recycled wood-framed storm windows. On sunny days he propped the lids open, and then closed them at night. Nowadays you can buy premade cold frames for under $100 that utilize sheets of twin-wall polycarbonate "glass" and aluminum frames.

I have built hot boxes that use fermenting horse manure to provide heat to a cold frame. Hot boxes have largely fallen out of favor, perhaps because good hot manure is hard to find. Horse barns now use so much bedding (and they clean stalls so often) that often there isn't enough manure mixed in to ferment well.

To build a hot box, dig a hole the size of your desired hot box and a foot deep. Line the sides with 2-inch-thick foam insulation to keep the heat from dissipating laterally. Fill it with steaming-hot horse manure. Then add 4 inches of topsoil to plant in. The bottom heat from the manure is great for germinating seeds and growing plants. The lettuces I planted in mid-April germinated quickly and grew well.

One word of caution: If the ground is too cold, the bacteria that produce the heat can go dormant. That happened to me once. I had to dig out all the manure and bring in another batch, which tempered my enthusiasm for starting earlier than mid-April.

Helping Plants Survive Tough Winters

By the end of February, I feel like one of those penguins in a French documentary as I walk the dog on cold nights in my many layers of clothing. Some of my plants are bundled up, too.

Trees and shrubs: In early January I wrap an old blanket or a piece of burlap around any young tree or shrub that is not well established, keeping it in place with string or a nylon strap. Then I spread some hay around the base to protect the roots from extreme cold. For small shrubs and roses, I crisscross cut evergreen boughs over and around a plant, then fluff up some hay and spread it on top. I've overwintered tea roses that way, which most gardeners assert are "definitely not hardy here."

Here's my theory: It's not just the cold that kills things, it's the wind, too. Whenever we get a strong subzero wind for a couple of days, I lose woody plants—or their buds. Fruit buds on my blueberries and blackberries get burned off by cold winds but survive the cold if it's less windy.

Soil Thermometers

Soil thermometers have steel probes attached to a dial that reads the temperature. I use mine in the spring to see when the soil has reached the elusive 60-degree mark that tells me it's okay to plant warm-weather crops. I use it to see if my compost pile is heating up properly. One winter when we had more than 3 feet of snow on the ground, I shoveled a spot in the vegetable garden to see if snow was the insulation it is claimed to be. It is. Only the top inch of soil was frozen, and 4 inches down the temperature was 39 degrees.

It's also my theory that the first three years of a tree's life are the most critical. Once a plant is well established, it'll do better than youngsters. So I pamper young trees and shrubs during the three-year break-in period. After that? They have to fend for themselves.

Perennials: I regularly grow perennials that are rated Zone 5 or warmer in my Zone 4 garden by finding just the right spot to plant them. A vigorous plant that has good soil, good drainage, and the right amount of sunshine is more likely to survive than one that is just limping along. Soil pH is also a key to success for some plants.

If your neighbor can grow lavender, for example, you can, too. Ask what your neighbor has done, and look at the site and soil. Consult a good reference text that tells about soil, moisture, and shade preferences for the particular plant you want to grow. It might mean that at planting time you have to improve drainage and sweeten the soil by adding limestone. Given all that, sometimes I fail anyway. I'm willing to try a perennial three times, and then, as in baseball, if I fail, "It's out!"

Final Thoughts

Vermont's weather may be cold and unpredictable, but Mother Nature has decorated the state with a fine selection of trees, shrubs, and wildflowers without any help from us. As gardeners we often choose plants that really don't belong here, from artichokes and hot peppers to tree peonies and wisteria. I'm as guilty as the next fellow: I want to be able to grow everything. If you want to, too, just remember that we won't always succeed. For your best chance of success, choose plants that are native to Vermont.

CHAPTER THREE

Water

When I was a boy back in the 1950s, nobody gave a second thought about turning on the sprinkler on hot August evenings and watering the lawn. I'd run through it, cooling myself while my parents rejuvenated the short, parched grass. Nowadays Burlington, Rutland, and most other towns with public water systems institute bans on watering—just when your lawn and gardens need the water most.

This chapter looks at factors that affect water needs, today's watering techniques, and ways you can conserve. Healthy plants with deep root systems can withstand considerable drought, and there is much one can do to help plants survive dry times.

Average Precipitation in Vermont

Vermont is blessed with fairly regular precipitation, averaging 3 to 4 inches per month year-round. According to National Weather Service data for the period 1971–2000, twelve weather stations reported an average of 43.24 inches per year. Totals ranged from an average of about 32 inches per year in Burlington and South Hero to a high of 54.3 inches in Peru. Mount Mansfield reported the highest, with an average of nearly 79 inches of rain per year.

Averages mean little, of course, if it's 90 degrees outside and your newly planted tomatoes are wilting. Watering can be critical for the survival of your plants. Water is the largest single component of plant tissue, and an adequate supply is necessary for success in the garden.

How Much Water Do Your Plants Need?

That's a little like asking "How many miles do you get per gallon in your car?" without asking what kind of car you have and how fast you drive.

Vegetables, annuals, and perennials: The rule of thumb for vegetables and annual flowers is that they need 1 inch of water per week—either from rain or from your hose. Some well-established perennial flowers might not suffer from a month of dry weather, but young tomato transplants might not survive three days of blazing sun without getting a drink. Roses are examples of plants that can survive without watering but that perform much better with regular watering. An inch of rain per week, or five gallons per plant per week, will increase the number of blossoms considerably.

Part of being a good gardener is being observant—and checking your garden regularly to see if plants need your help.

Trees: Mother Nature does a pretty good job of taking care of trees in the forest, and she will do so for you, too. But young trees are different. They need to be watered every week unless you are experiencing a very rainy time. A brief shower will not do the job.

Five gallons of water per week per tree is best. If you are

What Time of Day Should You Water?

Each gardener has a theory on the ideal watering time. Some say watering should be done early in the morning so that the sunshine will evaporate water off leaves, reducing the possibility of fungal disease. Others say water in the evening, so that moisture can soak down deep into the soil and not evaporate so quickly. Me? I say water when you have the time and your soil is dry. Pay attention to how your plants respond, and decide for yourself. It's not rocket science.

using a hose attached to a watering wand, time how long it takes to fill a five-gallon pail. For me, it's about a minute, but that depends on water pressure. Then watch the second hand or count to yourself as you water each tree. You'd be surprised how long it takes to deliver five gallons. Distribute water in a 3- to 4-foot circle around the tree, not just at the base of the tree. Do this every week the first summer of a tree's life at your house, and do it once a month the second year. And be sure that the soil around your tree is moist at the end of the growing season, before the ground freezes.

Lawns: Water needs for lawns vary according to soil type, grass type, and age of the lawn, among other things. A new lawn needs pampering while its roots develop. A well-established lawn shouldn't need watering except in times of drought. It is better to water deeply once a week than a little every day. One inch per week is generally accepted as adequate for most lawns.

Factors That Affect Water Needs

Type of plant: Each species of plant has a specific need for water. Cacti are renowned for going months without water. Cattails grow in swamps. Most plants are somewhere in between—they need that elusive "moist, well-drained soil" that garden books cite as best for everything from arugula to zebra grass.

Soil type: Soils differ tremendously in the amount of moisture they can retain. Sandy soils retain very little, while clay soils hold on to water so strongly that they often stay too wet. A good silt-based loam will retain water but allow excess to drain off.

If you have sandy soil, you have three choices: (a) grow plants with minimal water requirements, (b) improve the soil by adding compost and organic matter to retain more water, or (c) water like crazy. Clearly, the second option makes the most sense in the long run. Adding compost will improve wet clay soils by allowing excess water to drain and air to circulate, thus drying out the soil.

Slope: The slope of your garden matters, too. Imagine a parking lot on a hill. Turn on the hose and the water will run off quickly. Your soil acts the same way, even though you can't see it happening under the top layer of soil. Water in the ground is pulled downhill by gravity—unless it is captured and retained by soil particles or organic matter.

Sun and shade: The amount of sunshine your garden gets affects how much water it needs. A shady garden needs less water than a full-sun garden. Afternoon sun is stronger than morning sun and has more drying power.

Watering Techniques

Some gardeners prefer to water by hand with a hose (or even a watering can), supervising exactly how much each plant receives. Others like to turn on a sprinkler and forget about watering. There are devices to do your watering for you while you lie in the hammock with the *New York Times*—or this book. Here are some of your options.

Timers

If you are busy and are likely to forget about your plants, or if you'll be away for two weeks in August, buy a timer.

There are electronic timers and mechanical timers. If you have trouble getting rid of the blinking numbers on your VCR or microwave, buy a mechanical one. Timers can be set for a week's watering. You can have it water for an hour every day, or two hours every other day, or only—or never—on Sunday. They attach to the faucet where you attach your hose, and even the mechanical ones take a battery to run the clock. Buy the simplest timer you can. I once had one that could only be operated by nuclear physicists or MacArthur Fellows, and it didn't get much use.

Sprinklers

The simplest sprinklers are those that have no moving parts. These often look like a little brass animal (rabbit, toad, etc.) with a nozzle that sends a fine mist up in a circle. The rate of flow and size of the circle depends on the water pressure you establish when you turn on the faucet.

Then there are simple spinning sprinklers. Three arms rotate around a central pivot, sending water quite a distance in a circle.

A reciprocating sprinkler or "flip-flopper" has an arm 18 inches long with lots of little holes that send out a fine mist. Water pressure moves the arm, spraying a rectangle of lawn or garden. This type of sprinkler can be adjusted to spray a larger or smaller area.

Rainbirds are the Cadillacs of sprinklers. Rainbird is actually a brand name, but the term is used for all of them, just as the word "Kleenex" is used generically. A metal tripod 6 feet tall supports a rotating nozzle that can spray water long distances. Again, there are ways of controlling just what is sprayed and what is not, though regulating them takes some practice. If you use an overhead sprinkler, measure its output by placing tin cans in various locations to determine how long it takes to deliver 1 inch of water.

Soaker Hoses

Soaker hoses are hoses that leak. No, not like the one your puppy chewed on. These are designed to leak—or ooze, really. They come in rolls, some that you cut to length, others all set to go. They need to be pinned down with landscape staples to hold them in place, and then most gardeners cover them with mulch. Because soaker hoses release water slowly, they water only a very small area, an area just 1 or 2 feet wide the length of the hose. Installing them is labor intensive. Soaker hoses can be used anywhere but most commonly appear in perennial gardens, where they are more or less permanently installed, wending their way around the flowers and shrubs. They can be used in vegetable gardens, but they usually

need to be taken up and reinstalled every year to allow for tilling and planting.

The gardener at the Saint-Gaudens National Historic Site in my hometown uses soaker hoses—but without a layer of mulch. That way he can see when one breaks or malfunctions. The plantings are so close together that the plants hide the hoses.

Drip Irrigation Systems

Farmers and gardeners in California are masters at installing drip irrigation systems. Every garden center in California has all the parts you need to design and install a customized system. Parts are harder to find in Vermont, but you can get parts through catalogs if you wish. Gardener's Supply in Burlington sells complete kits with everything you need to set up a small drip irrigation system. Sprinkler Warehouse will sell you the components to design and build your own system of any size. See chapter 14 for contact information.

Basically, a drip system consists of 1-inch plastic pipe that can be punctured with a little tool to install small-diameter hoses and emitters. The emitters deliver water at a specified rate in gallons per hour, and you can distribute water exactly where you want it.

Watering Wands

I love watering wands. They attach to the end of the hose and consist of an aluminum pipe with a watering rose on the end that delivers a nice gentle spray. They have a bend near the end of the pipe to make the angle of watering comfortable, and a plastic grip insulates the pipe so cold water doesn't chill your hands.

I don't like watering every inch of the garden, walkways and weeds included. Because I have good soil and well-mulched beds, I prefer to water just the plants that are newly planted or that seem to need a drink of water. My watering wand allows me to walk down a row of tomatoes, for example, pulling the hose behind me, stopping to water each tomato plant but nothing else. By adjusting the water pressure with a valve on the watering wand, I can deliver water gently or send out a lot. The best brand I have found is Dramm.

Watering Cans

Every gardener should have a watering can. No need to buy a fancy metal one; plastic ones work just fine. They are the best way to water delicate seedlings that have just germinated, although a watering wand can be almost as gentle. Sometimes it's just less work to fill a watering can than to drag a hose over to a thirsty plant. Get one that has a handle from front to back, not side to side. That makes it easier to use with one hand.

What Can You Do to Conserve Water? Mulch!

Mulching is the easiest and best way to conserve water. A hard rain on bare soil is likely to run off, not only missing the chance to give your plants moisture but also removing some of your precious topsoil. Mulch helps to prevent runoff and to retain water that has penetrated the soil. Mulch also helps to keep down weeds that might otherwise compete with your plants for water.

Straw, mulch hay, or leaves: In the vegetable garden I use straw, mulch hay, or leaves. I let the soil warm up and dry out in the spring, then I put down a layer of newspapers (about six sheets thick) in the walkways and around plants. I cover the newspaper with 3 to 4 inches of mulch. I find that earthworms love newspapers, so most of the paper is gone by the end of the summer—adding more organic matter to the soil.

In the old days newspaper inks had toxic heavy metals that could accumulate in soils and be absorbed by plants. That is no longer the case. Inks today are soy based, even the colored inks. Unless your fingers get black from handling the paper, the newspaper was printed with soy ink and is safe to use around vegetables. If you are mulching the garden on a windy day, take the hose and wet down the papers before you try to spread them. Just run the hose into whatever type of bin you use to store the papers.

Leaves are the best mulch as far as I am concerned—both in the vegetable garden and the flower beds. I visited garden designer and writer Sydney Eddison in her Connecticut garden during a major drought several years ago and was amazed at her soil: It was moist, fluffy, and full of earthworms. Her secret? Mulching with leaves for thirty years or so. She uses leaves that have been run over by the lawn mower, which chops them into small pieces that decompose more quickly. She spreads the chopped leaves in the spring after all her perennials are up.

I rarely have enough leaves, but I save all I can. If your neighbors put theirs by the side of the road in bags for the town to collect, go get them! One word of warning: Ask your neighbors if they use pesticides of any kind on their lawn. If they used the lawn mower to suck up the leaves, you'll be getting grass, too, and you might be getting more than you bargained for: herbicides. I won't accept grass clippings from lawns that have been treated with "Weed-n-Feed" products.

Black plastic is used by some vegetable gardeners to control weeds and retain moisture. I don't like it because it looks ugly, creates water pockets for mosquitoes to breed in, and may negatively affect my soil microorganisms. I can't tell if the beneficial worms, bacteria, and fungi can survive and thrive in the soil under it, so I avoid it. I've tried it—it's an easy way to keep down weeds for large expanses of pumpkin patch—but I no longer use it.

Landscape fabric is a woven synthetic material that comes in rolls. This is best used under some of the mulches listed below. Water and air can pass through the fabric, but weeds cannot. The heavier types block out light, but the lighter ones do not. You need to buy special landscape staples to hold it in place. Landscape fabric is not ideal on steep hillsides, as mulch tends to slide off it and go downhill.

Landscape fabric can be effective for keeping out weeds but is labor intensive to install if you are cutting and fitting it around existing plants. New installations are easier: You cover your bed and then cut holes for plants. Some years later, as perennials or shrubs approach maturity, you may have to go back and cut away more fabric to allow plants to expand. Some weeds will eventually send roots through mulch and become embedded in the fabric itself, making the weeds almost impossible to pull.

Bark chips: Every garden center sells a variety of bark or wood chips. Chips are primarily used in flower beds and around trees—places that don't get tilled every year. Many garden centers also sell bark mulch in bulk, which is usually much cheaper than by the bag. I prefer fine chips as they spread more easily, look more natural, and break down into usable organic matter faster.

If you buy mulch in bags, read the labels. Avoid any that are "color-enhanced" as they have been colored with dyes Some less-expensive types are made by chipping wooden pallets or construction debris.

Cocoa mulch is very fine, nice looking, and smells like chocolate chip cookies for a week or two. I've found that it will often turn moldy in the heat of the summer, though that disappears after a while. It can be slippery when wet and tends to slide downhill in the rain. I've used it but don't like it. It's also expensive, and I've heard that it can be poisonous to dogs silly enough to eat it.

Pebbles or river stone: Lovely to look at, smooth round pebbles can effectively hold in moisture and repress weeds. But if there

Will Mulching with Bark Chips Steal Nitrogen from My Plants?

No, I don't believe so, though it is often said that it will. The theory is, and this is true, that the soil microorganisms that break down bark chips need nitrogen from the soil to build proteins as they multiply. But I've never seen any ill effects. Nitrogen-starved plants have yellow leaves, and as much as I've used bark chips, I've never had a problem. If you are worried, top-dress the soil with a slow-release organic fertilizer before you mulch. I always add some organic fertilizer and compost at planting time, which may be why I've never had a problem.

are lots of weed seeds in the soil, weeds will pop up in between the pebbles. You can get around that by putting landscape fabric beneath the stone.

Knowing When to Water

How can you tell when it's time to water? Sink your fingers into the soil. Yes, there are moisture meters, but you don't need one. Soil should be lightly moist. During droughts you might want to dig down 6 inches or more from time to time to see if moisture has penetrated.

Buy a rain gauge to see how much rain fell during the night or while you were at work. Remember, most plants do fine with an inch of rain per week. If you haven't gotten any rain in a week, check the soil to see if plants need watering.

Watch for signs of stress. A good gardener can see plants starting to stress long before the plants collapse. Leaves will lose a little of their turgor, or stiffness, as they get thirsty. Don't wait until plants wilt! By then they are almost ready for a trip to the emergency room. A constant supply of moisture keeps plants growing. When they wilt, plants are already shutting down their metabolic processes.

In hot weather plants grow faster and lose more water to transpiration, the plant equivalent of sweating. A newly planted broccoli plant might not need watering on a cloudy, cool day but will suffer without water if it's in full sun on a 90-degree day.

Final Thoughts

Knowing when and how much to water is not rocket science. If you have plants that are not thriving, do your homework: Read about them, or ask a knowledgeable friend. Each plant has specific moisture requirements. Remember that sloped gardens need more water than flat ones, that sunny beds need more than shady ones, and that clay holds water but sandy soil does not.

Put the right plant in the right place, and you shouldn't need to water much when plants are mature. Don't overwater. Soil nutrients can wash away with too much rain or too much watering. A good soil will hold moisture and keep a reserve for your plants, so work on improving your soil. And if you feel like it, run through the sprinkler on a hot summer evening. Your plants won't laugh at you.

Green Things

CHAPTER FOUR

Vegetable Gardening

A carrot just out of the ground, lightly rinsed with the hose; a sun-warmed 'Sun Gold' cherry tomato; raw pole beans just off the vine: These are the flavors I have used to teach my grandkids, George and Casey, about the joy of eating vegetables—and the value of growing them. I'm enamored of the whole process of growing vegetables—from planting the seed to eating the produce. I believe that if more Americans had vegetable gardens, there would not be an obesity epidemic. But growing vegetables is not just a way to eat well or to save money. Growing vegetables, for me, is a way of connecting with the earth that has provided for all of us for millennia. It is a joy.

Some gardeners hesitate to grow vegetables because they think it is too much work given Vermont's short growing seasons. Or perhaps they don't know where to begin, or remember the monotony of being forced to pull weeds as youth. Don't be daunted. Vegetable gardens are worth every moment you spend on them, and they need not take too much of your time. This chapter will give you techniques to make your life in the garden easier.

Starting a Vegetable Patch from Scratch

A vegetable garden will be with you for many years, so do a little planning before sinking spade into soil. Think about how much work you are willing to take on. Select a good site and prepare the soil properly so the garden will be a success.

Determine How Much Vegetable Garden You Need

Start small. There is nothing more discouraging than digging up the lawn to create a huge garden, only to find out that your first efforts are not as successful as you had hoped. Gardening is a learning experience, so you shouldn't expect to have a perfect garden the first year. And it takes time to build a good soil that will produce a good crop.

A 10-by-12-foot garden is a good start. This will give you room for two wide beds, 30 inches each, with a walkway down the middle and a little buffer zone between the garden and the lawn. One row could be for growing four tomato plants, with some room left for a few potatoes; the other would have space for carrots, beets, lettuce, and other favorites. Of course, you can plant just one tomato if you prefer, and set up a fence for climbing beans or early peas, or plant zucchinis and cukes instead of tomatoes. It's your garden and you can plant whatever you want.

Determine How Much Sun You Need

The more sun, the better. To grow leafy things like lettuce, you can make do with four to six hours per day. For tomatoes and pumpkins and peppers, eight hours or more is best. What if you can get only six hours of sun? Go for it. You'll still get tomatoes, just not as many.

Situate your garden away from tall trees—and not just because they will shade your garden. Their roots extend farther than you can imagine, and the fine roots that you might not even notice will be sucking up water and nutrients. Imagine a wine glass on a dinner plate. The glass is the tree, the dinner plate the roots.

Lay Out the Garden

I find symmetry pleasing—as do most people—and I want my garden to look good. It doesn't take much work to set up your garden so that it is neat and attractive. Whatever shape you decide on, grow tall plants like corn and tomatoes on the north side of the garden to minimize the shade they throw on shorter plants.

Use string and stakes to lay out the garden neatly, and use a tape measure if you want it symmetrical. If the angles are all 90 degrees for a rectangular garden, the diagonals will be equal in length.

Of course, if you prefer, you can lay out your garden in the shape of a half moon or a hexagon or a five-pointed star. Gardens should be pleasing in the eye of the beholder.

Remove the Sod

Do not, I repeat, do not, rent a rototiller and just chew up a section of lawn. That won't get rid of the grass. You must remove the grass, roots and all, or it will keep re-growing from the roots you've chopped up.

Removing sod is laborious, but less so if you have the proper tools. Do a little every day until it's done instead of working out at the gym, perhaps.

Buy an edging tool. This tool has a sharp crescent-shaped blade on a long handle. When you step on the edger, it slices through the sod to just the right depth. Cut the sod into squares or rectangles with the edging tool, tipping the handle back and forth to loosen the grass clumps. Pull up the sod with a garden fork or garden rake, or roll it up with your hands. Save the sod for your compost pile, or use it to patch bare spots elsewhere in the lawn.

There is a motorized device called a sod lifter that you might be able to rent if you are planning a 25-by-50-foot garden. It cuts the sod into strips, roots and all, so all you have to do is lug it away. For huge gardens, hire a farmer with a tractor and a moldboard plow. The plow will flip over the sod and bury it a foot deep, where it will slowly decompose.

Improve the Soil

Get your soil tested before you do much so that you find out the characteristics of your new garden's soil and what amendments it needs. See chapter 1 for details about soil tests.

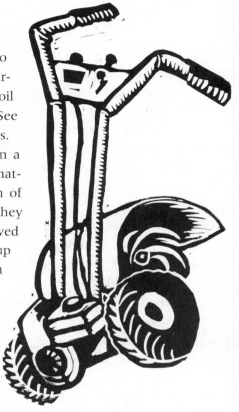

If your new garden has been a lawn, it may be low in organic matter and fertility. I'm not a big fan of rototillers, but for a new garden they make sense—once you've removed the sod, that is. They will loosen up the soil and allow you to mix in compost or aged manure. Rent, or if you're lucky, borrow one. In my opinion, it's not worth buying a tiller.

Start by rototilling a new garden twice, once right after the other. A metal depth guide on the machine allows it to stay near the surface or to go deep. If the soil is hard packed, start shallow. Then till again, going as deep as you can. Loosening the soil down to a foot deep is good if you can. Only rototill when the soil is dry—or at least not soggy. (See chapter 1 for a test that will let

Clean That Rototiller!

It is very important to clean the tines of the rototiller you've rented before you start, washing off any dirt in your driveway. You do not want someone else's weeds, diseases, or parasites to enter your garden.

you know if your soil is dry enough to rototill.) Preparing a new garden bed in the fall is a good way to get a jump on gardening in the spring.

The best thing you can add to your garden is good compost, but if you can't get enough, buy aged manure from a dairy farmer. Why not use fresh manure? Cows aren't efficient in processing the grass they eat, so viable seeds often pass right through them, meaning their fresh manure can introduce grass and weed seeds to your garden. Therefore, ask for the stuff that is two to three years old or, better yet, that has been "hot composted." Some farmers turn their piles of barn scrapings with a front-end loader to aerate them and get them "working" and hot—fermenting fast enough to heat up and kill the weed seeds. Manure is ready to use when there are earthworms in it.

Four to 6 inches of compost or aged manure mixed into your soil will greatly improve it. Ask if the farmer will deliver right to your garden, and then ask for delivery on a day when the soil and grass are dry so the truck won't get stuck. Spread out the compost and work it into the top 6 inches of soil, either by hand (with a garden fork) or with a rototiller.

Add fertilizer when you are ready to plant, rather than when you rototill. That way the nutrients will not be dispersed into the garden walkways or down deeper than roots usually go.

There are two exceptions: Add rock or colloidal phosphate and limestone or wood ashes before you rototill. Rock phosphate is slow to become available to plants, and it does not normally migrate through the soil the way most amendments will. Limestone and wood ashes are inexpensive and best distributed everywhere.

Vegetable gardens need some minerals replenished every year to ensure maximum veggie production, and new gardens generally need more help than established ones.

Instead of the traditional chemical fertilizers, I recommend organic bagged fertilizers for three main reasons: First, they release their minerals over time, which means the ingredients won't dissolve immediately and wash away the way many chemical fertilizers will. Second, organic fertilizers provide trace minerals and other needed nutrients that are not present in chemical fertilizers. Third, chemical fertilizers are made using petroleum products. A bag of 10-10-10 uses the energy equivalent of a gallon and a half of fuel oil. Multiply that by millions of gardeners to understand why we shouldn't use chemical fertilizers when there are good alternatives.

Warning: Don't get sticker shock! Organic fertilizers cost twice as much as chemical fertilizers, but they are worth it. As explained in chapter 1, greensand and rock powders are also good soil amendments. I add these when I plant, stirring them in with bagged fertilizer where plants will be going.

Raise the Beds

Use a short-tined garden rake, shovel, or hoe after rototilling to create raised beds that are mounded higher than the walkways. Beds should be 24 to 36 inches wide and 4 to 6 inches above the walkways—or higher. I recommend leaving the same raised beds in place year after year, merely adding compost or aged manure on top and working it into the top few inches. Leave walkways between the rows that are wide enough to walk on comfortably— and for your particular wheelbarrow.

If you have a problem with grasses or ground ivy creeping into your beds, you may wish to use boards to contain the beds and keep out creepers. Don't use pressure-treated boards, as they can leach toxins. Rough-sawn hemlock lasts well; if you use 2-inch-thick boards, they should last ten years. Even 1-inch planks are fine, they just won't last as long.

Why raised beds? Traditional narrow rows of carrots or lettuce assume the roots are all very close to the plants, but plant biologists now know that roots spread far and wide. The fine roots of veggies are so small we can't see them. Stepping on soil compacts it, making it less hospitable to roots, and causing root damage.

Wide raised beds allow you to grow more plants per square foot than traditional beds. Imagine a single row of carrots, a path, another row of carrots (or beets, or whatever), another path, and so forth. Wide beds allow you to avoid having so many paths, hence more room for veggies.

Lastly, raised beds reduce the chance that you, or your kids and dogs, will step on plants or the soil near plants. Your pathways are clearly defined with raised beds, even when plants are young.

Plant the Garden

Spacing seeds properly when planting will save you work later when it's time to thin out the extra plants. Small seeds are difficult to manipulate, so some gardeners pour them into one hand, then pinch and sprinkle them with the other. Other gardeners tear off a corner of the seed pack and try to pour seeds out slowly. Some folks buy devices that hold seeds and trickle them out slowly. None of those methods is perfect.

Each spring I start many of my vegetables and annuals flowers indoors in plastic six-packs and then transplant the seedlings outdoors after the last frost. That allows me to space plants perfectly. But when working with small seeds, it's often difficult to place just a seed or two in each cell. So I use a 6-inch section of a ¼-inch wood dowel sharpened like a pencil to help me. I place seeds in a bowl, then wet the tip of the dowel. When I touch a seed, the dowel picks it up like a magnet. When I touch the seed to the soil surface, it is released. You need to re-wet the dowel frequently. Sometimes I use this technique outside, too. It easily allows me to plant carrots an inch apart, reducing the need to thin later on—though I wouldn't want to seed a 50-foot row that way.

Planting depth is listed on the side of the seed packet, but as a rule tiny seeds should be right on the surface and big seeds in holes three times as deep as the seed is long. I'd rather be closer to the surface than too deep. For tiny seeds sprinkle some fine soil, vermiculite, or soil-starting mix over the seeds. Sometimes I do this by filling a kitchen sieve or colander with soil and shaking it over the seeds. Then I press down lightly with my hands, firming up the soil to get good contact between the soil and the seed.

Seed Choices: Heirloom versus Hybrid

In recent years gardeners in Vermont and elsewhere have been buying more and more heirloom seeds. These are seeds of varieties that your grandparents—or even *their* grandparents—might have grown. Heirloom plants are not bred for transporting long distances or for fitting into standard cardboard boxes, so commercial growers tend to avoid them.

The 'Brandywine' tomato may be the best-known heirloom of the lot. It is a big, awkward-looking, slow-to-produce, pinkish tomato that is also one of the best-tasting tomatoes I've ever eaten.

Hybrid plants are the result of carefully pollinating one variety with another to get new varieties that have the best qualities of each parent. In particular, hybrids are grown for disease resistance, size, looks, and transportability. And many of them are excellent plants. Don't save seeds from hybrids—they won't breed true, and you probably wouldn't like what you get. You may wish to try some heirlooms and some hybrids, too.

Open-pollinated plants are those that are not hybrids. You can save seed from these plants, but some—such as those in the squash family—are a bit promiscuous and need to be kept away from their cousins if you plan to save seeds. If not, you'll get hybrids that might not be very tasty when you grow the seeds next year.

What about seeds from genetically modified organisms (GMOs)? GMOs are much in the news these days. GMOs are made when scientists insert genes from one species into a non-related species to confer resistance to herbicides or to produce built-in biological insecticides. Corn, soy, and other field crop have been developed as GMOs, but as far as I know, GMOs are not being sold to the home gardener with the exception of some sweet corn from Monsanto or Siminis Seeds. The cost of developing GMOs is very high, so seeds for most vegetables might never be produced.

Starting Seedlings Indoors

When I was young and too busy to mess around with seedlings in early spring, I bought seedlings at the local greenhouse. Later, lured by luscious color catalogs that offered varieties of tomatoes and peppers that I couldn't find as seedlings, I started growing my own. Now it is one of my joys in life: starting unusual things indoors when winter feels like it will go on forever. I recommend it. Again, start small—one flat or two. I now start 300 seedlings or more each year, but I've had lots of practice.

What do you need? Lights. Buy 4-foot, two-tube fluorescent shop lights. A table in a cool room, preferably by a window. Temperatures 65 degrees during the day and cooling to 55 degrees at night are ideal. Plastic six-packs for individual seedlings and plastic flats (trays) to contain them. Be sure the flats are the kind that hold water (some have slits for drainage). Sterile potting or starting mix.

To Start Indoors or in the Ground?

Due to Vermont's short growing season, some plants must be started indoors or purchased as seedlings at a greenhouse that has done the work for you.

Here's a list of those that should be started indoors early and when to start them indoors for a Zone 4 garden (for colder or warmer locations, adjust the dates by a week or so as appropriate): artichokes (2/15), Brussels sprouts (3/1), broccoli (3/15), cabbage (3/15), cauliflower (4/1), eggplants (4/1), leeks (3/1), melons (4/1), onions by seed (3/1), peppers (3/1), tomatoes (4/1 to 4/15), and watermelons (4/1).

Others can be planted indoors to get a head start, including asparagus from seed (3/1, it's usually planted by root), beets (3/15, though rarely done), cucumbers (4/15), kale (3/15), lettuces (3/15), melons and pumpkins of all kinds (4/1), spinach (3/1), squashes of all kinds (4/1), and swiss chard (3/15). These also can be sowed directly outdoors later.

Everything else? Plant seed directly in the ground. Read the seed packets for timing.

Optional: a heat mat designed to be placed under a flat to warm seeds and speed germination. Enthusiasm.

Hang the lights over the table, about 6 inches above your seedlings. Hang the lights from something that will allow you to raise them as the plants grow. I hang mine from the ceiling, but I also have a plant stand with adjustable shelves. If you use the ceiling, get toggle bolts to hold the weight, as screws will eventually come out of drywall, wreaking havoc below. I use jack chain (a metal chain available at hardware stores) to hang the lights.

Some people start a few plants on the windowsill. What they get, however, are usually tall, spindly plants that are struggling. If

A Few Words about Seed Companies

I joke that the seed companies have spy satellites to see who needs their catalogs. Once you're on one list, it seems that you're on everybody's list. I like ordering seeds from New England companies like Johnny's Selected Seeds of Winslow, Maine, and High Mowing Seeds of Wolcott, Vermont. High Mowing is all organic and carries many heirloom varieties. Fedco Seeds of Maine is a cooperative, and its prices are low. Baker Creek Heirloom Seeds is a good source for old varieties. The Cook's Garden and Renee's Garden Seeds both have some wonderful varieties I can't find elsewhere. Seeds of Change sells organic seeds only, including many flower varieties. West Cost seed companies like Nichols Garden Nursery and Peace Seeds have some unusual and wonderful seeds you won't fine elsewhere. You'll find these companies listed in chapter 14.

you try windowsill gardening, keep the plants as close to the glass as possible, as the sun's strength dissipates quickly as you move the plants back from the window. Better yet, if you don't have lights, start plants like tomatoes indoors later, in early May. Put them outside in the sunshine during the day as soon as temperatures allow (above 50 degrees). The bottom line? Vermont's sun in the spring really isn't strong enough to do the job. Get some lights.

Six-packs for planting come in various sizes, from thirty-six cells per flat to ninety-six. Go for bigger cells to allow more room for roots to grow and to keep the cells from drying out so quickly.

The standard way of starting seedlings is to use sterile potting mix, which is a peat moss–based planting medium. Fill the six-packs with mix and add water. The mix will be very dry and probably resist getting wet; fill the flat partway with water and let the mix suck it up from below. That might take an hour or more. Or wet the whole bag of planting mix the day before.

Make a small divot in the planting mix with the tip of a pencil or a sharpened dowel and drop in a seed. I actually make two divots and add two seeds to ensure that at least one germinates in each compartment.

To get good contact with the mix, add more soil mix and press down lightly on it with your fingers after planting. For tiny seeds I don't make a divot but place the seeds on the surface and sprinkle a fine layer of vermiculite on top. Vermiculite is heat-expanded mica sold as fine powder to hold water in sterile planting mixes. Read the package as some vermiculite comes in bigger chunks, which doesn't work for this.

It's critical that your seeds not dry out while they are waiting to germinate or when the seedlings are very young. The best way to prevent desiccation is to cover the flat with a clear plastic cover. These are sold along with the flats and, unlike the six-packs, can be reused each year. Some folks use plastic wrap or even a plate of glass to keep in moisture, but if some seeds germinate and send up tall seedlings while others are still snoozing, you have a problem. The clear covers will let the early birds get a couple of inches tall while waiting for late starters. If you see mold start on the surface, take off the lids.

You can use anything for starting seeds: old margarine containers, yogurt cups, etc. Some gardeners like peat pots, but I do not: They tend to dry out faster than plastic. Others make pots of used newspapers wrapped around a form—but that is too much work for me.

After germination, I take scissors and cut off the smaller of the two seedlings. The sooner you do this, the better. If they get too big, they're competing with each other and both suffer—and you'll be tempted to keep both.

Soil Blocks: Another Way of Starting Seedlings

If you're tired of buying sterile potting mix and those little plastic six-packs every year, there is an alternative: soil blocks. These are 2-inch cubes of soil, compost, and minerals made with a simple metal press available from seed companies like Fedco and Johnny's Selected Seeds. In recent years I've been using this technique, and I like it.

Most gardening books warn against using real soil when starting seeds because they say fungi in the soil could cause a disease called damping-off. Damping-off makes seedlings literally keel over and die, and there is little one can do to stop it. Using sterile mix minimizes the chances of that happening.

There is another way of looking at the situation, one that I prefer. I believe that using garden soil and compost introduces *beneficial* soil organisms in your planting blocks, helping plants to be healthy and resist disease. If you have good air circulation, adequate light, and a growing medium rich in nutrients, you should have plants that will succeed, not succumb. I've never lost seedlings to damping-off when using soil blocks.

Here's what I do: Using a two-quart plastic juice pitcher, I measure out ten quarts of dry peat moss, put it in a wheelbarrow, and mix it with one quarter cup of limestone (to counteract the acidity of peat). Then I add three quarts of coarse sand, ten quarts of peat humus (available in bags at garden centers), and one-half cup each of the following: colloidal phosphate (or rock phosphate), greensand, organic blood meal, and rock dust or Azomite (optional). I mix well, then add ten quarts of compost and ten quarts of rich garden soil. Some people eliminate the sand and peat humus; others add more sand than I do. This recipe makes enough for 300 to 400 blocks, but you can make a smaller batch—or share with your friends. The sheer messiness of this might make a good school project!

To start my block making, I mix four quarts of the dry ingredients with one quart of water in a small plastic tub, stirring it with my hand (wearing a rubber glove). I add more water until the mix is gooey but firm, not watery.

To make blocks I create a pile of the gooey stuff 4 to 5 inches deep, then compress it by pushing down on it with the block maker. When the mix fills up the four cavities of the blocker, I get rid of any excess by rotating the blocker as I push down against the bottom of the tub.

The tool ejects the blocks with the squeeze of a spring-equipped handle. You can drop them right into a plastic flat, which is just the right width for the block maker. One flat holds eight rows—for a total of thirty-two blocks. Later you can water the blocks by adding water to the flat and letting the blocks suck it up. Dip the block maker in a bucket of water after each squeeze of the handle to clean it.

The great thing about making soil blocks is this: Roots stop when they come to free air, so the young plants don't get root-bound the way seedlings do in six-packs. At planting time the block goes into the soil, and the roots are not disturbed. A 12-inch tomato plant in a plastic cell of a six-pack has severely tangled roots that need to be teased out at planting time, which causes delays in growth until it recovers. The same size tomato plant grown in a block has roots ready to grow immediately.

Hardening Off Seedlings

You wouldn't fly to Miami in February and spend a day at the beach without hat or sunscreen. Nor should you take the seedlings that you've pampered indoors for eight weeks and suddenly put them outdoors in full sun and wind. Plants need hardening off, a process to get them toughened up to the sun and wind.

Start by carrying your seedlings outdoors and putting them in a place sheltered from the wind and where they can get a few hours of morning sun. The north side of the house is generally good for that. Bring them inside before the afternoon sun reaches them. Do that for a couple of days, then give them some afternoon sun, but water first if they are at all dry. Finally, let them stay out all afternoon and then have a sleepover, staying out all night. Be sure to bring them in if the temperature is going to get close to 40 degrees. I take an entire week to harden off my plants—but I may be an overly protective parent.

When to plant those hardened-off seedlings? A cloudy or drizzly day is best. Late afternoon or evening is better than morning, as your plants have time to settle in before exposure to a hot sun.

Weeding

Sometimes gardeners get discouraged because the weeds take over. There are many solutions. First, start small. If you rototill a section of lawn to start a garden, that rototilling will not kill all the grass and weeds, and they will return. It's best to dig out the turf to start a garden.

Consistency is important, too. Just as you probably make your bed each day, or wash the dishes, or take a shower, you need to include weeding as part of your daily routine. If you can spare 10 minutes a day, it will make a huge difference. Weeds compete with your plants for water, nutrients, and (if they get big enough) sunshine.

Little weeds are easier to remove than big weeds. Loosen the soil with a hand weeding tool and they'll come out with a gentle tug. Grasses invade garden beds by sending long roots in, but can be deterred by "edging" the bed. That means creating a V-shaped moat around the bed. When invading roots hit open air, they stop growing.

I like the CobraHead Weeder, a hand tool shaped like a curved finger. It has a sharp widened tip that can slice off weeds or tease out their roots. By pulling it through the soil, you can lift portions of roots that might have broken off when you pulled out a weed. With this tool you can loosen the roots, and pull from below while tugging the top of the weed with the other hand. See Chapter 11 for more discussion of weeding tools.

A good layer of mulch will prevent many weed seeds from germinating. See Chapter 3, which discusses the various options. Mulching your walkways and open places will save you hours of hoeing down weeds. Mulch right after a thorough weeding.

Lastly, never let your weeds flower and produce seeds. Once seeds get into your soil they will bother you for years to come. Of course some seeds will blow in, keeping the tidiest gardeners weeding regularly, no matter what. Try to learn to enjoy weeding, or at least the results—neat, tidy garden beds.

Planting Tips by Vegetable

Artichokes: Start seeds indoors in February, or buy seedlings. The artichokes you'll get will be much smaller than those from the grocery store, and each plant will give you just three to five. But they are pretty plants. They like full sun and rich, moist soil.

Asparagus: Buy roots at the garden center and plant them 4 to 6 inches deep. Add rock phosphate and organic fertilizer to the soil, plus lots of compost. Water regularly the first year for best success. Or you can start asparagus as seeds and save money. Don't eat any the first year, just a few stems in year two, and be moderate in year three. Never pick for more than four to six weeks.

Beans: Before you plant, buy some rhizobial bacterial powder. The powder needs to be purchased fresh each year for best results.

This will inoculate the plants with nitrogen-fixing bacteria, which will improve your soil. Moisten the seeds and sprinkle the powder on them. The same procedure goes for peas. And pick beans regularly to keep them coming.

Beets: Each "seed" is actually a seed capsule with two or more seeds, so you will have to thin them after germination no matter how carefully you spaced them. Do so when leaves are 4 to 6 inches long and eat the thinnings.

Broccoli: Plant early and late. Start some seeds indoors and plant seedlings in mid- to late May; plant seeds again in late June for a fall harvest. Don't plant when the soil is cold and wet— that will encourage cabbage maggots. The same goes for cabbage and others in the brassica family. Row covers are good for keeping off pests that affect broccoli and cabbage, such as flea beetles and cabbage worms. If your seedlings are leggy at planting time, plant them deep, covering up stem but not leaves.

Brussels sprouts: These are highly frost-resistant in the fall, but not so much in the spring. I pick until Thanksgiving or later. Cut the tops off your plants on Labor Day weekend to get the sprouts to get big. Deer love these, especially after the first snow.

Carrots: The seeds are tiny, and hard to space, but if you don't thin, your crop will not be good. Now pelletized seeds, which are bigger, are available in many catalogs. Side dress the carrots with an organic fertilizer on the Fourth of July, and scratch it in for bigger carrots.

Celeriac: This is a good substitute for celery, and it stores well in the fridge for months. Start early by seed, or buy plants. They need lots of water and rich soil.

Cucumbers: Grow them on a trellis to save space. I start them by seed indoors, and plant them outdoors when the plants have true leaves and are big enough to survive cucumber beetles that can eat seedlings when they first come up out of the ground. Row cover also helps with the beetles.

Corn: Don't crowd your corn or you will get smaller ears. Plant corn in blocks of 4 rows, 30 inches apart; plants in the rows should be 8 inches apart. Avoid supersweet varieties—Vermont soil is usually too cold at planting time. I start my corn indoors in 98-cell plug trays on June 1 on a heat mat. They germinate in three days, and I plant them as plants too big for the crows—in about ten days. More work, but better results.

Garlic: Plant cloves in October and cover with 12 inches of straw or mulch hay. Garlic will grow through the mulch in spring, but weeds won't. Harvest when the flower stems (scapes) curl and lower leaves start to brown up. That will be in late July or early August. Save the best bulbs for planting next year.

Horseradish: A little goes a long way, and never goes away. Plant by root where you can contain it with a lawn mower, as it spreads.

Leeks: These are easy. Buy plants or start seeds indoors early. Plant in a trench and fill it in as the plants grow. That will give you more white stems. Plant with plenty of compost, and keep moist.

Lettuce: Plant seeds every two to three weeks from May to September 1 and you'll always have plenty.

Melons: Melons and watermelons are tough to grow in Vermont, but if you put out big plants and pick the right variety, you can get a few. Some gardeners grow them on black plastic for more heat and to control weeds.

Onions: Starting onions indoors from seed early in March is better than growing them from sets (little bulbs) planted outdoors in May. There are more varieties of seeds to choose from, and plants started from seed are more vigorous. Cut back seedling tops by half after six weeks indoors. Outdoors you should plant onions where your soil stays the most moist, not in a dry raised bed. Water in dry times, and know that onions hate weeds. Some seed companies sell bundles of started plants, which is a good way to start them.

Parsley: Soak seeds in very hot water for an hour or more to help them germinate faster. I often buy seedlings as it's easier.

Peppers, eggplants: These guys like it hot. Grow them under row covers until they flower. Even then, eggplants don't need insect pollinators, so they can stay covered. Chunks of dark rock placed near them absorb heat, helping them to stay warm at night. Peppers grow well crowded together, say 12 inches apart.

Potatoes: Cut seed potatoes into chunks, each with an eye or sprout, and let the cut surfaces dry for a day or two before planting. I use a post hole digger to dig holes 6 to 8 inches deep for planting. Potatoes grow roots below the chunk you planted and your potatoes above, so add compost and organic fertilizer in the hole and stir, then plant—cut side down. They need 6 inches of soil over them to grow lots of spuds. As the shoots grow, fill in the hole to increase production and hill up the bed with soil from the walkways as they grow.

Pick a Peck of Peppers

The late Marguerite Tewksbury of Windsor operated an organic market garden for more than sixty years. When growing peppers, she warned against adding fertilizer to the soil: "That way, peppers won't turn into trees, which they're so apt to if you fertilize them—you get trees and no peppers," she told me. She scratched in wood ashes around the plants when they bloomed and again in late August, and she got great production.

Marguerite Tewksbury froze sliced, unblanched peppers for use in winter salads. She just took a few slices out of the freezer when she was ready to toss the salad and they were still crunchy when eaten right away.

Spinach: This is a cold-weather crop, so plant it early or late. Most varieties bolt when it's hot.

Squash: These are easy! Follow the directions above for cucumbers.

Sweet potatoes: This is a hot-weather crop. Vermont gardeners can only grow them successfully under black plastic in rich soil. They need plenty of moisture, so some kind of in-ground watering system is recommended. I grow them under row covers and hoops for added heat.

Swiss chard: Plant seedlings 6 inches apart, or by seed. The more you cut it, the more it grows new leaves, but leave a few when you harvest. The roots taste like beets if boiled at the end of the season.

Tomatillos: Easy to grow, but you need both male and female plants, so plant a few. They take up a lot of space.

Tomatoes: It's common to have tomato plants that are tall and leggy when it's time to put them in the ground. You can turn all that extra height into roots by pinching off the lower leaves and planting your seedling sideways. That's right, just keep the top cluster of leaves and plant the seedling in a trench, not a hole. Turn up the top so the leaves are just out of the ground—the stem is flexible and won't snap. Don't give tomatoes too much fertilizer or they will grow tall with lots of leaves, but fewer fruits.

Thinning Seedlings in the Garden

Imagine if your mother had given birth not only to you but also to eleven other siblings all at the same time. Imagine what it would be like if you all had to live in the same house and survive on the same amount of food your parents bought every week when you were growing up. That's what some unlucky lettuce, abused beets, and cruelly crowded carrots go through every year. Some gardeners cannot bear to thin their seedlings or don't have the time—and shame on them!

Thinning plants is critical to success in the garden. Vegetables compete with each other for sun, moisture, and nutrients just the way they compete with weeds. Thin early in the season, as soon as you can get your fingers on the young seedlings. You can transplant thinned seedlings—even beets and carrots—if you wish and if you have space.

Scissors are great for thinning. Just snip off seedlings at ground level when they are young. It doesn't disturb the roots of developing plants the way pulling them out might.

Geo's Favorite Vegetable Varieties

For the past ten years, Geo Honigford has been growing vegetables alongside the White River in South Royalton. He sells his certified organic produce at the Norwich farmers' market and directly from the farm. His vegetables, blessed by good alluvial soil and a yearly dose of aged manure, are beautiful and bountiful. He grows everything from A to Z (asparagus to zucchini). Here are some of the varieties Geo likes, with a few of my favorites thrown in for good measure:

Acorn squash—'Table Ace'

Asparagus—'Jersey Knight' (Geo plants it by seed.)

Beans, bush—'Easy Pick' (Geo plants several times to harvest beans all summer.)

Beans, pole—'Kwintus'
(My pick; it produces
all summer and
stays tender even
when large, and
it freezes well.)

Beets—'Golden Beet',
very large; Red
Ace; 'Chioggia', a
sweet striped beet
(my pick)

Broccoli—'Arcadia', 'Gypsy'

Brussels sprouts—'Oliver'

Butternut squash—'Waltham'

Cabbage—'Farao' (green),
'Ruby Perfection' (red)

Carrots—'Sugar Snax'

Cauliflower—'Violet Queen'
(purple)

Celery—'Conquistador'

Corn—'Ruby Red', a popcorn; 'Delectable' (butter and sugar)

Cucumbers—'Olympian'

Eggplant—'Orient Express', 'Black Bell', 'Neon'

Kale—'Winter Borer' (My favorite, too!)

Leeks—'King Richard'

Lettuce—'Waldmanns' (green leaf), 'Vulcan' (red leaf), 'Salad
Bowl' (oak leaf), 'Sun Devil' (iceberg), 'Ermosa' (Boston),
'Red Cross' (red Boston)

Melons—'Early Queen'

Onions—'Copra' (yellow, great keeper), 'Frontier' (early yellow),
'Red Wind' (red, huge)

Parsnips—'Lancer'

Peppers, sweet—'King Arthur', 'Ace' (it ripens early to red), 'Islander' (purple), 'Labrador' (yellow)

Potatoes—'Russian Banana' (fingerling), 'Yukon Gold', 'Butte' (russet, for baking), Purple Peruvian (blue), 'Red Pontiac' (my pick; a red-skinned white flesh potato)

Pumpkin, carving—'Howden'

Pumpkin, pie—'Baby Bear' (one- to two-pound size, right for one pie)

Radishes—'Altaglobe'

Radishes, fall—'Red Meat' (my pick; plant them August 1; very sweet, nice even when huge)

Spinach—'Tyee'

Summer squash—'Multipik'

Sweet potato—'Beauregard' (from Fred's Plant Farm, 800-550-2575; or Johnny's Selected Seeds, 877-564-6697)

Swiss chard—'Bright Lights'

Tomatoes—'First Lady' (Geo's favorite red tomato both for slicing and canning), 'Sun Gold' (cherry, one of my favorites, and very prolific), 'Brandywine' (my pick for heirloom slicer)

Watermelon—'Sunshine' (yellow)

Winter squash—'Buttercup', 'Blue Hubbard', 'Red Kuri'

Zucchini—'Raven' (I like 'Romanesco', a ridged fruit that is good eating even when large.)

Not every one of Geo's picks will be right for you. Try new varieties and ask your neighbors what works well for them.

Final Thoughts

If I could only grow one vegetable, it would be the cherry tomato 'Sun Gold'. It starts early and produces seemingly limitless numbers of little nuggets of flavor. I dry them in our electric dehydrator and use them all winter in soups, stews, salads, and even sandwiches. They remind me, especially on snowy days, that the gardening season will be back before too long.

Veggies that you grow yourself taste better than those from the store. And if you decide to grow them organically, you can eat them knowing no chemicals were used to produce them.

CHAPTER FIVE

Eating from the Garden All Year

Winters are long in Vermont, but even so you should be able to eat something you grew in your garden every day of the year—and you don't have to quit your day job to do so. A garden that is 20 feet by 30 feet in full sun can produce a huge amount of food. If you plan properly, and understand the best ways to freeze, dehydrate, and store food, you can eat something from the garden every day. This chapter will teach you all you need to know to keep your garden produce tasty all year

I once went 20 years without ever buying a potato. During that time I ate them regularly from late summer to spring, then in early summer I planted my garden with the sprouting potatoes I had left over in my cold cellar. I didn't eat potatoes again until the new ones were edible-sized "new potatoes." The first ones I harvest each year I get without digging up the plants. I just slip my hand under flowering potato plants and grab some small spuds for a real treat: new potatoes after two months or so without eating any potatoes.

Eating seasonally is how our great-grandparents got by one hundred years ago. But now we have freezers and food dehydrators, so eating from the garden is easier for us than it was for them.

Storage

Storage is the best, least expensive way to keep food. But you need to pay attention to temperature, humidity, and rodent control to avoid losses. Let's start with those potatoes.

Potatoes store best between 35 and 50 degrees, with high humidity. Commercial potato growers keep them in storage right at 50 degrees because at cooler temperatures some of the starches turn into sugars, making them darken when turned into french fries—which is how most commercial potatoes are used. Because I generally eat mine boiled or mashed, I like a potato that is a little sweeter.

I have an old refrigerator in the basement, one that was built before "frost free" became the standard. It is great for storing potatoes, carrots, rutabagas, beets and celeriac. The "new-fangled" fridges are constantly changing the air and removing moisture so that there will be no frost build up—but they dry out vegetables except in the vegetable drawer. My old fridge, which was manufactured in 1946, works great and is perfect for storing root crops like potatoes that need high humidity. I set the thermostat at its warmest setting and it uses little electricity.

You can use a newer, frost-free fridge if that is all you can get. Your potatoes will shrivel a bit over time, and carrots will get a little soft, but a fridge will keep the mice out, and will keep your produce cool if you have a heated basement (mine is quite cold, and I don't heat it). Keep your produce in plastic bins in the fridge, and cover each bin with a damp cloth that you moisten from time to time.

One alternative is to build a "cold cellar" or a "root cellar," which is really just a bin made of cement blocks with a plywood lid that you build in your cellar or garage. When I have too many potatoes for my storage fridge, I store my root crops in 5-gallon pails in the cold cellar. I put an inch of clean sand in each bucket, along with a little water for the humidity.

Temperature can be hard to control in a cold cellar. In the garage the temperature may drop below freezing in January. In the cellar, especially near the furnace, it may be too warm. Raising the temperature is easy. I use a heat mat inside, the kind I use under my trays of seedlings in the spring. Or you can use a 60 watt light bulb in a drop light inside your concrete box to keep the temperature above freezing in cold times. But too warm? Bringing in outside air would do it, but would require some engineering skills on your part.

So what should you store in your cold cellar or spare fridge? Beets, carrots, celeriac, kohlrabi, leeks, parsnips, potatoes, rutabagas, and turnips. But for long term storage I find that freezing is better for beets and leeks (more on that later), and that parsnips store best in the ground. I eat parsnips after the snow melts, my first spring treat from the garden.

One word of warning: Apples would store well in the cold cellar, but they give off a gas that promotes ripening in other fruits and vegetables. So if you want to store apples, you should keep them away from other veggies. Don't mix apples and spuds in your cold cellar.

Building a Simple Cold Cellar

To build a storage space for potatoes and other root crops to winter-over in, you will need twenty standard cement blocks (each 16 inches long by 8 inches wide), a piece of plywood about 32 inches by 64 inches in size, and half an inch thick. Measure your bin before cutting your plywood.

This bin will hold six to eight 5-gallon pails. Place your blocks with three on each side and two on each end. Stack your blocks two high and cover the top with plywood. I find the plywood tends to warp, so you will need to put something heavy on top—mice love potatoes and carrots, and can squeeze through very small places. I didn't use mortar between the blocks, but you might want to.

Low Humidity Storage

Winter squash, onions and garlic need to be stored in a cool environment, but with low humidity. The best place for them is in a bedroom upstairs with the heat off and the door shut—that should keep things around 50 degrees and quite dry, which is perfect. An old gardener told me that he stored all his winter squash under the bed in the guest room.

Onions need to be well dried before storage, or you risk having them rot. The best technique is to dry them outside in the summer after harvesting. I do it on my deck where they get good breezes, but not a lot of sun. I rotate them from time to time so that all sides get exposed to the summer breezes. After the tops have totally dried, cut them off about two inches above the onion and the onions are ready for storage.

Not all onions store well. Plant yellow storage onions like 'Copra' or 'Patterson' if you want onions all winter. Even with those, watch for rot and use any with soft spots first.

I have a wooden rack with a dozen slotted drawers for storing onions, garlic, and small winter squash. The racks are designed so that air can circulate. I got mine from Gardener's Supply (www. gardeners.com). They call it their Orchard Rack.

Garlic should be harvested in July or August when the leaves start drying out. Don't cut off the tops right away, as there are nutrients in the tops that will flow back into the bulbs as they cure. Let the tops dry in a cool, airy barn or garage for a week or more to dry out before storing. I like to tie garlic in bundles of ten bulbs and hang some of them in the kitchen. The kind of garlic we can grow in New Hampshire, stiff-necked garlic, doesn't lend itself to braiding.

Warm Storage

Some years I've had great luck growing sweet potatoes. These need to be stored warm and dry. Never put sweet potatoes in the fridge, or keep them in a place cooler than 50 degrees. Properly stored I have kept them all winter and spring. A basket in the kitchen, perhaps, is the best place. But like any stored vegetable, watch out for rot.

Freezing

If you are serious about eating your garden produce all year, you need a freezer. Chest freezers are the most efficient in terms of energy use, but I like an upright freezer because I can see what is in there more easily. It's easy to lose track of things stored near the bottom of a chest freezer, and food loses its flavor and quality if stored more than a year.

I have an old freezer that requires me to defrost it once a year, and a newer one that does not. I recommend the frost-free type even though they are a little less energy efficient. Defrosting is a lot of work that can be avoided.

Blanching

Many vegetables have enzymes that promote ripening of seeds and general aging. Unless you drop them briefly in boiling water to kill those enzymes—a process called blanching—they may get woody or tough. Knowing how long to blanch your vegetables is very important. Boil them too long and you'll have mushy beans or zucchini. In my experience a brief blanching—just a minute or so—is perfect.

It's worth buying a blanching pot if you want to freeze vegetables. This is really a two-pot system: an enameled tin pot to hold water and a second interior pot that is full of holes that you fill with vegetables. I fill my outer pot, complete with its inner section, roughly half full of water and bring it to a rolling boil. Then I drop my veggies into the water and time how long they are in, while watching them change color. Vegetables like beans, broccoli, and kale will noticeably turn a lighter, brighter green when they are adequately blanched.

Generally sixty to ninety seconds of blanching is all that is required, even though the water may not even return to a full rolling boil. Use lots of water and not too many veggies for a quick return to boiling. Vegetables should still be crunchy, not mushy, when they come out of the hot water. Brussels sprouts take a little longer in the hot water because they are larger and denser than most veggies.

But taking veggies out of the hot water is not enough. You need to cool them quickly in a cold water bath. I lift the inner pot, let if drain into the cooking pot, then use the lid to catch any drips as I carry it to the kitchen sink. I've already filled the sink with cold water, and I drop the veggies in for a few minutes to cool them quickly. I drain them, and spin them in my salad spinner. I like the kind of spinner that has a pull string (mine is a Zyliss brand). Finally I spread them out on a cloth tea towel and blot them with another towel. They are then ready to go in freezer-grade zipper bags. Freezer-grade bags cost a few pennies more than storage-grade bags, but are much better for the job. I always use new bags for freezing, not ones I've washed and recycled.

To Blanch or Not to Blanch?

What should you blanch? Beans, beets, broccoli, Brussels sprouts, carrots, cauliflower, corn, kale, spinach, squash, and swiss chard. What does not need it? Apples, berries, pears, peppers, leeks, and tomatoes do not need blanching, in my experience. Tomatoes, beans, and Brussels sprouts freeze well whole, the others I cut up. Summer squash freezes well in half-inch cubes and is a great addition to winter soups. Winter squash I often steam or roast, then scoop out of the skins and into bags.

When freezing vegetables it's a good idea to remove as much air from the bags as possible. There are machines sold that will do so, but I just use a common drinking straw. I get the bag closed around the straw, suck out the air, and then snap the bag shut as I pull out the straw. The bag should cling to the vegetables if done right.

Tips for Freezing Specific Vegetables

Tomatoes are wonderful frozen whole. Just clean them and be sure they are dry before packing them in zipper bags. No need to blanch them. Suck the air out, as described above. Then, when you need tomatoes for a stew, soup, or stir fry, just take out a few "red rocks." Freezing ruins the consistency for sandwiches or salads, but when thawed, the tomatoes you froze will be like canned tomatoes.

If you wish to remove the skins, just run the frozen tomatoes under hot water from the sink and rub. The skins come right off. Or you can drop them in a bowl of hot water for a couple of minutes, which will also speed up the thawing. I freeze some cherry tomatoes, and add them right to the cook pot without bothering to remove the skins.

Leeks can be stored in the fridge, but they take up a lot of space and lose character with time, so I freeze them. Cut off the roots and the tops of the leeks, then slice lengthwise. I chop them into half-inch pieces and put them right in the bags. They are great for winter soups, and as a substitute for onions if you run out.

Apples freeze well. I like to freeze them in bags containing the right quantity for making one apple pie. You can even freeze them in a pie pan, and after they are frozen you can remove the pan and put the frozen apples in a two-gallon zipper bag. Applesauce and cider are also a treat in winter, so I freeze both. My local orchard is willing to make cider from apples I bring, and they will bottle it in half gallon jugs, which fit on the door of my freezer. I tell them I am freezing the cider, and they leave enough air space at the top, so the cider won't spill when it expands as it freezes.

Frozen berries are great for adding to hot oatmeal in winter or cooking briefly to make a sauce for ice cream. I freeze blackberries, blueberries, elderberries, raspberries, and strawberries. Sometimes I spread them out on cookie sheets before freezing, and then package them when they are frozen hard. But if I'm in a hurry—or feeling lazy—I just pack them in bags and freeze them. That seems to work fine. Be sure to cut off the attachment points on strawberries before you freeze them, too.

You need to remove all those little stems on elderberries before freezing them; I recently learned that you can hold the cut stem of a bunch of berries and whack them against an old tennis racket. The berries come right off and sail through the racket.

Beets freeze best when peeled, cut into bite-sized chunks, and then blanched for two minutes instead of one.

Peaches? A friend has both 'Reliance' and 'Red Haven' peach trees that produce well at her home near the Connecticut River. She blanches the peaches by dropping them in boiling water and keeping them there until the water re-boils, and then counting to 10 before taking them out. She says the skins slide off easily after you drop them in cold water. She suggests pitting and slicing them, and freezing in a solution of water and lemon juice to keep the color from browning. She uses 1 tablespoon of lemon juice per quart of water. She freezes the peaches in plastic containers made for food.

Peppers do not require blanching, and keep their character well after freezing. You can take a few slices out of the freezer and add to a tossed salad. By the time you eat the salad, they will be thawed but not soggy.

Roasting

Tomatoes and peppers (both hot and sweet) can be roasted in the oven—or even on a grill. Roasting sweetens these vegetables and takes out some of the water. Most people remove pepper skins after roasting, though that is a lot of work. I generally cut tomatoes in half and roast them on a cookie sheet at 350 degrees in the oven. This caramelizes the sugars, and makes them less bulky to store. I put them just one layer deep in a gallon freezer bag that I place on a cookie sheet until frozen. I use them in winter in sandwiches. I take out a few slabs of roasted tomatoes and cook briefly in my toaster oven to thaw them before putting in sandwiches.

Dehydrating

Drying food in a dehydrator is a fine way of concentrating flavors and saving space. I regularly dry tomatoes, hot peppers, apples, and pears. I've dried carrots, squash, blueberries, and other foods, but find I don't bother with those most years. Dried food can be stored in zipper bags in a cool pantry, in the fridge, or in the freezer for long-term storage.

Food dehydrators vary considerably in price and efficiency. My favorite, after trying several kinds, is the Excalibur (www. excaliburdehydrator.com) with nine large square trays. I like it because the heating element and fan are behind the trays of food, blowing across them sideways. This means all the fruit dries at the same rate. All others I've tried have the heating element and fan at the bottom or at the top, and there is uneven drying—the trays nearest the heater dry first. Still, there are others available at a fraction of the price. It is the most efficient in terms of electricity use that I have used. It uses 666 watts per hour.

The Excalibur's main competition comes from NESCO American Harvest (www.nesco.com). They have a couple of nice dehydrators that come with eight trays, and either bottom or top heat. I prefer the one with bottom heat, even though mine has no timer. I used both kinds for several years. Both use 1000 watts of energy per hour.

When drying food, temperature is important. The lower the temperature, the longer drying takes, but it's better for the vitamins, particularly vitamin C. I generally dry foods at 125 to 130 degrees to minimize nutrient loss.

I dry tomatoes, apples, and pears to the point where they are dry, but not brittle. Chewy is good. Hot peppers I dry until brittle, and then I grind them in my coffee grinder. That allows me to sprinkle on a little zing to a dish—or a lot.

Canning

Entire books have been written about canning. I still can a few jars of tomatoes every year, but it is hard work, and if you do it wrong you can get very sick. So I will let an expert tell you how to do it. My suggestion is *Putting Food By* by Greene, Hertzberg, and Vaughan.

Final Thoughts

One of the joys of having a vegetable garden, for me, is eating good food, food that I know has never been sprayed with chemicals. I love using my own garlic and tomatoes in January, or taking a bag of berries out of the freezer in April. Yes, it does take time, but if you prepare foods for the freezer or dehydrator in small batches on a regular basis, it doesn't seem like too much work. And if your tomato or pepper crop fails, or doesn't produce enough for your winter needs, most farm stands will sell produce to you by the bushel at a very reasonable rate.

CHAPTER SIX

Annual Flowers

In much of Vermont, gardeners flock to garden centers just before Mother's Day to buy annual flowers in bloom: common ones like marigolds and petunias and lesser-known greats like nemesia, diascia, and scaveola. Planted on a warm Sunday and covered up on cold nights that threaten frost, these flowers will bloom until well after Labor Day.

Annuals are flowers that live out their lives in a single season. Unlike perennials (which normally survive the winter and return in spring), annuals must produce lots of flowers—and seeds—to start another generation, one that will bloom the next year. To be sure they will have offspring, most annuals keep producing flowers all summer if you give them what they need. And they are great in containers.

Every gardener should grow annuals, says Liz Krieg of Bethel. She specializes in growing annuals, and her business provides annuals wholesale for use in containers and window boxes, as cutting flowers, and as fillers for every nook in the landscape. She starts many by seed, and she buys plugs (little seedlings) of trademarked specialty flowers. I consider her the Queen of Annuals—though perhaps I should call her the Cheerleader of Annuals. I don't think she's ever found one she didn't like or couldn't grow.

Krieg rightly points out that annuals easily provide great, bold colors all summer long. Unlike perennials, they will put on a great show their first year, reaching maturity and blooming like crazy. "They're instant gratification," she says. "You can buy them in bloom, plant them, and keep them blooming and getting better all summer long." She is my advisor when it comes to annuals.

Starting Annuals by Seed

There are lots of wonderful annuals that you can start from seed, which saves you money and enables you to get varieties that a small, neighborhood farm stand might not have. And if you have the time and space, you can grow a hundred of one kind of flower to use in Cousin Connie's wedding—or just to make arrangements to give away.

It makes sense to start most annuals in the house instead of sowing seeds directly into the soil outdoors. Vermont weather being what it is, most annuals need a head start or their blossoms won't show up in your garden much before Labor Day. Liz Krieg warns against starting them too early, however. Seedlings that have been in the house too long are usually spindly or root bound.

Read the seed packets carefully to see how long each variety of flower takes to germinate, and plan to plant seedlings outdoors six weeks after germination. Return to chapter 4 and follow the directions for starting vegetable seedlings.

Selecting Good Seedlings

Don't feel guilty if you'd rather buy young plants than start seeds. Not everybody wants to germinate annuals in the house and tend seedlings for two to three months. Vermont's greenhouses produce a bounty of bodacious hanging planters, scores of kinds of six-packs, and plenty of small pots with flowers ready to follow you home. But be forewarned: Bigger isn't better.

Many annual flowers in six-packs are already in bloom in garden centers by the time you are ready to buy them. Each cell in those six-packs has very limited soil, and big plants often have big root systems—roots that are so tangled up from growing in the small cell that they won't expand unless you tease them out with a finger or a tool. Even so, the root-tangled plant may just sit there for a while, recovering and doing nothing. That's not good for Vermonters who have a short growing season.

Educate yourself. If you plan to buy plants, talk to knowledgeable friends, read the gardening magazines, and make a list before you go to the greenhouse. Instead of just buying what's in bloom, buy small plants of things that will be gorgeous later. Seed catalogs can be great reference guides, too.

Where should you buy seedlings? I strongly recommend that you buy your seedlings only from family-run garden centers, farm stands, or at your local farmers' market. Local folks carry varieties that do well in our climate and know how to grow them.

In contrast, plants that have been shipped halfway across the country may have dried out in transit and suffered root-tip dieback that you can't detect, but that will hinder growth all summer long.

Or somebody who means well (but works the rest of the year in hardware) may overwater plants in the Big Box store until they develop root rot. Locally grown plants are almost always good.

Care and Feeding of Annuals

Fertilizers: Annuals vary a lot in how much fertilizer they need. Many of the old classics like zinnia and cosmos get awfully tall and bloom later if given fertilizer. But new varieties often do better with regular fertilization—they've been bred for container growing and expect a dose of chemical fertilizer every two weeks. But you don't have to use chemical fertilizers. All I do is add compost and a slow-release organic fertilizer to the soil at planting time, and my annuals do fine. Or I will water with a diluted dose of fish and seaweed fertilizer in mid-summer if my annuals need a pick-me-up.

Watering: Annuals usually have smaller root systems than perennials, so most need to be watered more often. Big annuals in small pots can barely make it through an August afternoon without a drink of water. Don't wait until your plants droop before you water them.

Liz Krieg recommends buying some hydro crystals to use when planting containers. These synthetic polymers, she says, are the same ones used in disposable diapers! They absorb water and release it to plants as needed. Just follow the directions on the packet, mixing the crystals in near the bottom of planters. These can be highly effective in keeping thirsty container plants healthy in hot weather, but I do not use them in the ground.

Pinching: Despite what you were told in kindergarten, pinching is good. When growing annuals from seed, pinch off the growing tips when the plants are 3 to 4 inches tall. Each pinched stem will bush out with three to five new stems. Pinch those back a month later, and the plants will bush out even more. You can use scissors or shears to cut off the growing tips on bigger plants.

Deadheading: If annual bachelor buttons have brains, they only have one thing on their minds: sex. They want to grow up and produce more bachelor buttons. Which makes sense: If they don't set seeds, their lineage will die out when the frost comes. Unlike perennials or trees, each annual gets only one chance to reproduce.

Your job, if you want annuals to bloom all summer, is to cut off the spent flower heads—deadhead them—as soon as they are bedraggled and before the plant thinks it has made enough seeds to start the next generation. That said, there are plenty of annuals that have been bred to keep on blooming even if you don't deadhead them. They are called self-cleaning. Ask at your local greenhouse.

Using Annuals

To fill in the garden: Many perennials take a year or more to reach full size, so new flower beds sometimes look pretty empty: a few perennials spread out on a sea of bark mulch.

Enter the annual. After planting your perennials, get some six-packs of annuals and pop them in the ground. Annuals are much less expensive than perennials and will get big fast and look good all summer long. Often you can buy a dozen annuals for the price of one perennial. But leave 8 to 12 inches between your annuals so they have room to grow without pushing and shoving each other like second graders in the lunch line.

In containers: Gardeners have been growing plants in pots at least since the times of Queen Hatshepsut of Thebes, Egypt, who reigned from 1504 to 1482 BC. Ancient wall paintings show clay pots being used to transport trees that produced myrrh, a fragrant resin. The mutiny on the HMS *Bounty* occurred on a voyage carrying breadfruit trees in pots to the West Indies to start plantations producing cheap food to feed slaves.

If you buy a hanging planter or fancy pot full of gorgeous blossoms, you must keep fertilizing the container all summer long. Container plants need a light, fluffy growing medium so that air and water can get to roots, but they also need lots of nitrogen. The commercial potting mixes used for growing flowers in containers are fluffy but are mostly peat moss and perlite, which have little or no nutritional value. Your plants will need fertilizer added every two weeks.

How Much Root Space in a Pot Does Each Plant Need?

A 6-inch cube of soil is ideal. Many containers potted up by nurseries pack a lot of plants into a pot to make it look good so you'll buy it. But later, as the plants grow, they are too crowded and they suffer. If you make up your own window boxes or pots, leave space for plants to grow. That way plants won't use up all the water so quickly in hot weather. Bigger plants need more space. Deep containers are the way to go, and self-watering containers help if you have a busy lifestyle and can't always water daily.

Instead of fertilizing with a chemical fertilizer, you can water with a liquid fish or fish and seaweed fertilizer. This will give your annuals micronutrients in addition to the N-P-K (nitrogen-phosphate-potash) found in chemical fertilizers. Or you can scratch a little bagged organic fertilizer on the surface of the soil mix from time to time.

Annuals in containers are often given foliar fertilizers. These are water-soluble fertilizers that are sprayed on leaves. I use a one-quart hand sprayer with a teaspoon of Neptune's Harvest fish and seaweed fertilizer mixed in with the water to give a little boost to plants in pots that are looking tired or neglected. It lets them know I love them—and provides a little extra nutrition.

The Classics

Some gardeners turn up their noses at the best-known annuals because they've "been there, done that." Not me. There are good reasons why marigolds and zinnias are popular, and if you haven't grown them, you should. Many old favorites have new varieties you might not know about. Here are a few of my favorites.

Alyssum or sweet alyssum: A low-growing white, peach, pink, or purple flower loaded with hundreds of tiny blossoms. They start easily from seed, I'm told, but I buy six-packs. Plant them 8 inches apart. They will bloom all summer and into the fall, surviving some frosts. Their fragrance is said to repel deer and attract beneficial insects that eat aphids. None of the deer I've tried to interview, however, have been willing to comment—so alyssum's repellent qualities may be mythical.

Marigolds: Not only are they bright and cheery, they are thought to offer certain repellent qualities—to predatory bugs, but that may be just a tale. It is known that the roots exude a chemical that will kill nematodes, a type of worm that can eat the roots of plants (though plenty of other nematodes are benign). You can plant marigolds by seed after danger of frost or indoors a month before that. Average soil is fine; don't bother fertilizing.

Nasturtiums: Plant these sprawling beauties in ordinary or poor soil, as rich soil or added fertilizer will produce lots of leaves but few flowers. Idea: Plant nasturtiums over daffodils to hide the foliage. The seeds are large, so they are easy for kids to handle. All parts of nasturtiums are edible, and you can even pickle the buds or green seedpods and use them like capers. The spicy flowers are great in salads.

Petunias: Even though standard, old-fashioned petunias are getting elbowed out by newer hybrids, they are still good plants. They should be started indoors eight to ten weeks before last frost. The seeds are small, but some companies are selling pelletized seeds for ease of handling. Pelletized seeds are coated in a fine clay to make them bigger.

Snapdragons: These flowers are perfect for cold-weather climates: They don't need hot summers and will survive light frosts in the fall. Ask a child to watch when you squeeze on the sides of a blossom: The mouth opens just like a dragon's. Start seed indoors in April or buy seedlings. Cut off any flowers at planting time, and deadhead regularly. Picking flowers encourages bushiness, too.

Sunflower: No longer just big, tall plants that produce bird food, sunflowers now come in many sizes and colors. They get their name from their obsession: the sun. Plant seeds outdoors after danger of frost. Most won't bloom until the late summer days get shorter, so buy day-neutral varieties if you want earlier results. Day-neutral varieties are not affected by day length. If you plant them against a wall, their faces will always look out at you. In the garden, they will face the sun.

The multiheaded varieties are the best bang for the buck, and they make great cut flowers. I love 'Teddy Bear' for its fuzzy yellow blossoms on short

Latin Names

You will notice that some Latin plants names are used in this chapter and again in the chapters about perennials and trees. Don't worry about pronunciation: Every letter is pronounced, and even the experts don't agree on how to pronounce *Clematis*, for example. Common names can vary from state to state, but Latin names are precise—the same all over the world.

Latin names consist of two words. The first is the genus, which is like your family name, Jones, for example. All your relatives also have first names, but in Latin we put that second. Some Latin genus names are also the common name, such as *Delphinium*. The second name is called the species name; in general species don't interbreed. If they do, their progeny are called hybrids.

To make things even more confusing, "hybrid" is a term also used to describe plants created by crossing different varieties or cultivars of the same species. The words "cultivar" and "variety" are used pretty much interchangeably. The main thing to remember about hybrids is that they won't breed true, so don't save their seeds if you want the same type of plant next year.

If several species of a genus are described in writing, the genus name can be abbreviated as its first letter only. Thus *Lobelia cardinalis* is spelled out for a first mention, then *L. splendens* and *L. siphilitica* for its cousins. If you want to refer to all the species of *Lobelia*, you can write *Lobelia* spp.

A note for Rodney Dangerfield: If you learn a few Latin names, you'll immediately get some respect from serious gardeners.

stems (and for the name), as well as all of the red/mahogany-petaled ones like 'Moulin Rouge' and 'Velvet Queen'. Get a seed catalog and drool over the sunflowers in February. Some are pollen free, which means they won't drop yellow pollen on your tablecloth.

Zinnias: Great cut flowers, these range in size from 3- or 4-foot giants (Benary's series) to 12-inch plants great for ground cover or containers (Profusion series) and everything in between. I love a lime green one called 'Envy' (as in green with . . .) or 'Benary's Giant Lime'—both are standouts as cut flowers. If you buy seedlings, get the smallest plants you can, as the bigger ones don't transplant well. And the more you pinch and cut the stems, the more flowers you get. There are some called 'Cut and Come Again' zinnias, which is precisely what they are!

Containers

Growing and thriving in a container is not easy: Conditions are usually hot and dry, with limited nutrients in the soil. Some annuals do better than others. Here are Liz Krieg's recommendations, in order of preference.

Surfinia petunias: These workhorses bloom all summer long and are cold hardy to 28 degrees. They have more flowers than other petunias, and the blooms appear at the top of the plant. They are self-cleaning, which means you don't have to deadhead. They come in a rainbow of colors, and as singles or doubles. They are short plants, just 6 inches or so, but their long stems can grow 3 to 4 feet long. Their disadvantage? They are trademarked hybrids, so you have to buy plants, not seeds.

Million bells or *Calibrachoa*: These plants are great for use as fillers. Although they like full sun, they will bloom with just four hours of sunshine. They are cold hardy and self-cleaning, blooming from early in the season to after frost. They can get up to 24 inches tall and come in a rainbow of colors.

'Purple Queen' *Setcreasea*: Liz loves these for the bicolor leaves: purple on top, green on the bottom. The stems are a foot or so long, trailing nicely over the edges of containers. She calls them great accent plants.

Iresine: Another great foliage plant, this one has bright cherry-red leaves. It forms a mounding plant 2 feet tall and wide.

Nemesia: These have blossoms the size of a dime that provide nonstop color in white, blue, purple, pink, and even yellow. The 'Sachet' and 'Serengeti' series are very nice, with plants up to 12 inches wide and 6 to 7 inches tall.

Zinnias, Profusion series: These are like baby zinnias, because they reach only 8 to 12 inches tall or so. Apricot, white, cherry, and orange are common colors. They'll produce all summer. In big containers, Liz also uses full-sized zinnias.

'Diamond Frost' *Euphorbia*: This delicate-looking plant is tough as nails. Tiny leaves, a mounding habit, and miniature white flowers give it an airy look. It does best with lots of sunshine. You can overwinter this one in the house and replant next year. It combines well with nemesia and grows 12 inches or more wide and tall.

Scaveola: My pick for a plant that blooms well all summer and recovers from drying out due to neglect (I know, and shame on me). Its sprawling stems carry true blue flowers. Scaveola is somewhat frost hardy.

Great Cut Flowers

If you want flowers in vases all over the house, plant a patch of annuals just for that purpose. Don't worry about garden design—just take over a part of the vegetable patch in full sun. Or tuck the plants in anywhere. "There's always room for annuals," Liz Krieg says. Below are her favorites, pretty much in her order of preference.

Zinnias: Krieg particularly likes the Benary's series, which offers large blossoms on stiff stems that hold up well in summer heat. They grow 40 to 50 inches tall in many colors. Refer to the "Classics" and "Containers" sections of this chapter for more about zinnias.

Larkspur is an annual delphinium. Krieg starts larkspur indoors in a very cool room and crowds the seedlings in small flats. She divides the seedlings in mid-May, planting them outside into cool soil in her Zone 4 garden. Plants will self-sow. Larkspur grows 36 to 48 inches tall and comes in blues, pinks, white, and purples. They need support to keep stems from flopping.

Cosmos plants are easy to start from seed at the same time you start tomatoes indoors. They come in heights from 16 to 48 inches, colors from the classic pink to yellow, and with many different petal shapes.

Lupine is actually a fast-growing perennial that Krieg treats as an annual. She picks the stalks as soon as the flowers begin to bloom, cutting them right to the ground. This eliminates the aphid and mildew problems that so often plague this species. Lupine grows 24 to 36 inches tall in shades of red, blue, white, and yellow.

Cleome or spider plant: "So long as you don't mind the cat-pee smell of the flowers, these are great. Architecturally wonderful," Krieg comments. Some have prickly stems. Cleomes are big plants: 36 inches tall and wide in pinks, purples, and whites. 'Senorita Rosalita' is a new, small cleome that stays under 2 feet tall and compact.

Brazilian verbena (V. bonariensis) offers small purple flowers on nice stiff stems up to 48 inches; it attracts monarch butterflies, too. "It is wiry and tall. You can get that airy purple mist effect in your garden as well as in vases," Krieg says.

Salvias: 'Gruppenblau' is the best variety, with deep blue blossoms on tall stems above handsome foliage. Krieg says it blooms at least a week earlier than other varieties and has more stems than the beloved 'Victoria'. Drought resistant, it likes poor soil and grows 24 to 30 inches.

Strawflowers: Use these sunburst-shaped blossoms fresh or dry. Colors include deep red, pink, purple, orange, and yellow. Blossoms are an inch wide on 24- to 36-inch stems. To dry the flowers, pick stems before the blossoms are fully open.

Snapdragons: 'Rocket Mix': This cultivar comes in yellows, reds, pinks, and white on plants 24 to 36 inches tall. Snapdragons are somewhat frost hardy.

When and How Do You Pick Cut Flowers?

Pick in the morning before it gets too hot or at dusk. Bring a plastic bucket or one of those tall, narrow metal picking buckets full of water to the garden. Plunging flower stems immediately into deep water prolongs the blossoms' vase life. Let them rest in the water for an hour or more if you pick them in the heat of the day.

Recut the stems when you make an arrangement, but remember the five-second rule: No more than five seconds should elapse from the time you recut a flower to the time it goes in the vase.

Cut flowers will last longer if you change the water and recut the stems regularly. Mix up a gallon of "flower power" water by adding a tablespoon of sugar and a drop or two of bleach, and use it in your vases.

Tender Perennials Used as Annuals

If you've moved to Vermont from California or from below the Mason-Dixon Line, you may know the following plants, but you probably consider them perennials. Not here. These need to be dug up in autumn and brought inside or they will die come winter.

Bedding geraniums (*Pelargonium x hortum*): Chances are that your grandmother grew red geraniums. Mine did. You can start these from seed in mid-February or buy plants in May. I bring geraniums into the house each fall and keep them as houseplants. Cuttings taken in April will root in water.

Dahlias: Because of the short season, Vermont gardeners often get dahlia blossoms only in September. Many of the big varieties take 120 days or more to bloom. But there are early, mid-season, and late-season varieties. You can start the small types from seed in February and get blossoms by midsummer. 'Harlequin' mix, 'Phantom', 'Figaro', and 'Opera' all work from seed. Buy tubers of 'Park Princess', 'Bonne Espirit', 'Red Cap', or 'Yvonne' for early blooms. If you want to grow dinner-plate dahlias, start tubers in pots inside in early April and transplant outside in June.

At the end of the season, dig up tubers a week or two after frost and bring them inside. Pack the tubers in slightly moist sphagnum moss or bark mulch in paper bags and store at 50 degrees.

Fuchsias: These come as both sun-loving and shade-loving varieties that are commonly used in planters. They are not generally started as seed. You can winter these over in a cool (50 degrees), dark basement. Cut them back by half in the fall, then let them dry out and go dormant. Bring them up into the house and start watering them in April. Or overwinter them in the house as a houseplant.

Annuals for Fragrance

Donna Covais is a horticultural therapist who grows mountains of flowers and vegetables in a tiny strip of land between her driveway and the house she and her husband, Joe, rent in Burlington. Twice she has won citywide prizes for her garden—and yet Donna Covais has been completely blind since 1995. Because she cannot see her flowers, she likes to grow flowers with nice scents. These are her favorites:

1. Alyssum
2. Heliotrope
3. Marigolds
4. Scented geraniums, particularly lemon scented

5. Peacock orchid (*Acidanthera*), a bulb plant, not an orchid
6. Annual dianthus
7. Sweet peas (see the sidebar)
8. Lemon verbena
9. Basil
10. Stock
11. Lavender
12. Petunia ("the smell of the garden, of summer")

Tasha Tudor's Tricks for Growing Sweet Peas

Tasha Tudor, the reclusive illustrator and icon of the simple way of life, lived in southern Vermont, not far from Brattleboro until she passed away in 2008. I had the opportunity to interview her twice in her later years and to visit her wonderful gardens. She shared her house with a corgi, a rooster, and a variety of small birds in a cage. For a while she even had a pet garter snake that took naps with her! She loved gardening and did some every day in season, even in her nineties.

Tasha Tudor loved growing sweet peas. She started them inside in late winter or early spring, as early as February.

When the soil outdoors was no longer soggy, she transplanted the seedlings in the garden in a foot-deep trench lined with manure. As they grew, she filled in the trench. Later on she fed them manure tea every two weeks.

I asked her to what she attributed her good health, energy, and long life. She answered without a moment's hesitation: "Goat's milk and gardening." She paused briefly and added with a straight face but a twinkle in her eye,

"And choosing the right parents."

Foliage Plants

I grow some of my favorite annuals not for their flowers but for their leaves. These beauties are always in bloom—which is to say their leaves are a treat to look at. I love their bright colors and shiny surfaces.

Elephant ear (*Colocasia esculenta*): The huge leaves of this tropical plant look indeed like elephant ears. It comes in green or purple, and it loves wet locations. Plant elephant ears in full sun with moist soil and it will delight you. It's expensive, so dig up the tuber in fall and store in a cool, dry place until spring.

Licorice plant (*Helichrysum petiolare*): I buy some of this every summer because I love the silvery leaves, because it mixes so well with bright colored flowers in planters, and because it takes abuse. It rarely complains even if I let it totally dry out. It flows over the edges of containers and weaves its way through other plants. It's an exceptional accent in flower arrangements. There are also lime green and chartreuse cultivars.

Perilla (*Perilla frutescens*): This terrific purple-leaf annual self-sows exuberantly. Pinch off the flowers (which are not at all showy) if you don't want it to self-sow and come back next year. It gets 18 inches tall. The 'Magellanica' hybrid has pink and green mixed in, too.

Persian shield (*Strobilanthes dyerianus*): This plant just shimmers with silver overtones on dark purple and pink leaves. It loves hot weather and gets big: One plant can spread over a 3-foot circle and stand 3 to 4 feet tall.

Sun-loving coleus: Long used as a colorful foliage plant for shady nooks, new strains developed in the 1990s do well in full sun. Colors range from deep crimson to brilliant chartreuse and golden sunset orange. Some plants have three or more colors on a single leaf. They like rich, moist soil and need to be 2 feet apart if planted in the ground.

Vines

Annual vines are great for growing through climbing roses and on archways and trellises. Here are some good ones.

Morning glory: It's best to start these directly in the soil, as they don't like being transplanted. Soak seeds overnight in warm water. Hummingbirds love the blossoms. They grow in full sun and average soil.

Passionflower (*Passiflora* spp.): There are 400 species in this genus, including some with very dramatic blossoms. Because it isn't easy to start from seed, buy plants and grow them in full sun once the soil and air are warm. Passionflower is a vigorous grower. Many species are perennials in warmer climates.

Purple hyacinth bean (*Lablab purpureus* or *Dolichos lablab*): This fast-growing vine has glossy dark leaves and pink-purple flowers that are edible, as well as the beans. Very striking.

Scarlet runner bean: Red-orange flowers and edible beans grow on this vine that will climb 15 feet or more in a single season.

Annuals for Shade

Shady corners need more than green ground covers to come alive. Here are some bright, easy flowers for shade.

Begonias: There are two types, wax begonias (*Begonia semperflorens*) and tuberous begonias (*B. tuberhybrida*). Wax begonias have masses of small flowers and waxy green leaves. Tuberous begonias have much more dramatic blossoms—larger, with peaches, reds, and bicolors readily available. Neither is easy to start from seed. Tuberous begonias need to go dormant in winter, so dig up the tubers and store them in a paper bag in a cool closet. Wax begonias in pots make nice houseplants for the winter.

Browallia: This beauty comes in violet and purple, contrasting nicely with impatiens. It needs rich, moist soil and suffers badly if

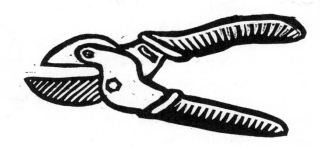

you plant it in a pot and don't water it regularly. It has 1- to 2-inch trumpet-shaped flowers, and hybrids are available with either cascading or bushy habits.

Edging lobelia (*Lobelia erinus*): Annual lobelia is sold everywhere in six-packs and most commonly has small intense blue or purple flowers. It will grow in full sun to full shade, but it tends to go dormant in midsummer. Fix that by cutting it back by one-half as soon as it starts to look ratty, and it will re-bloom until frost. Don't let it dry out!

Impatiens: This is the best-known flowering shade plant and a surefire favorite because it will bloom continuously all summer with little care. You will need to buy plants, as it is not easy to start from seed, but you can make more plants by taking

Don't Yank Those Dead Annuals

Instead of pulling out your annuals after frost, snip them off at ground level. When you pull them, you leave loose soil for weed seeds to land in and bare soil that can wash away in heavy rains. However, roots left undisturbed will decompose and give organic matter back to the soil. Pull them in the spring when you plant.

cuttings and rooting them in water. Impatiens likes rich, moist soil and will grow in full shade to part sun.

Unfortunately, since 2012 there has been a fungal disease called impatiens downy mildew that has devastated plants in Vermont. Experts warned that once the disease got into your soil, your chances of growing impatiens in the future were slim. Signs of the disease? Flowers and leaves drop off, leaving bare stems, almost as if slugs had eaten them. There is no cure, and if your plants develop the disease, pull them and put in the household trash. Even our cold winters do not seem to kill the fungus. I have had good luck growing impatiens in pots with new potting soil.

New Guinea impatiens is not susceptible to the disease, nor is SunPatiens, a trademarked hybrid. Sunpatiens, as the name suggests, needs some sun but will tolerate some shade, too.

Torenia: This is relatively new to most nurseries. It is a plant good for sun or shade, and has been offered as a substitute for impatiens. I've had good luck with it in shady locations. It is low-growing and comes most often in shades of blue, or in white.

Lesser-Known Greats

Not all great annual flowers are well known. Be the first on your block to try these three beauties.

Angelonia: A bit like a snapdragon, this comes in white, pink, dark purple, and blue. It likes heat, is drought tolerant, and allegedly is not interesting to deer. Height: 12 to 24 inches.

Gaura: This is a perennial in Zone 5 and warmer, but don't depend on it. It has wonderful pink, almost orchidlike flowers growing all along long stems that tend to sprawl. 'Siskiyou Pink' is a nice cultivar. Height: 24 to 36 inches.

Twinspur (*Diascia* spp.): Originally from South Africa, this is a smaller plant with creeping stems and upright flower stalks with small, trumpetlike flowers. Great in containers, it doesn't like hot, dry locations. A perfect cool-weather plant. Height: 6 to 12 inches.

Final Thoughts

Annuals, in the plant world, are like the brass section of an orchestra. They've got to be a bit brash if they are to survive. They must attract a pollinator this year—or a plant grower who will save their seeds or who will bring them inside the greenhouse until next summer—otherwise there will be no next year for their genetic material. So their colors are intense, and they bloom and bloom and bloom. Annuals really try hard to be your friends. Don't be turned off by the fact that you have to start some every year. They are worth the effort—and the price.

CHAPTER SEVEN

Perennial Flowers and Bulbs

Having a garden with a diverse collection of perennials and bulbs is a bit like having a birthday every week from spring until fall. There are always new surprises in my garden: In March it's the snowdrops pushing through the frozen soil, followed by an array of other spring bulbs—scilla, crocus, daffodils, and tulips— through April and beyond. In May the subtle colors of hellebores and primroses delight me every day. June brings peonies—many of them fragrant—and the Siberian iris that contrast so nicely with them. And so on each week until late October, when colchicum and fall crocus bloom and decorate the table.

You, too, can grow perennials and bulb plants that will surprise and delight you. Perennials are available that will grow almost anywhere, and most really are remarkably trouble free. If the soil, moisture, and sun conditions are right for them, perennials will share their glory with you for years.

What Do Perennials Need?

At least five factors are important in getting a perennial to perform well and come back every year: amount of sun, type of soil, pH of the soil, amount of moisture held in the soil, and lowest temperatures of winter.

There are limits, of course. You can grow a desert plant in Vermont, you just can't grow it in a bog. Sun lovers will survive in the shade, they just don't bloom as much or get so big. Even plants that would rather be living in the "tropics" of Pennsylvania can be grown in the Green Mountain State—as long as the other four conditions for success are met.

Sun: Sun-loving perennials need six hours of direct sunshine per day for best results, and preferably more. But four hours of afternoon sun will suffice, or six hours of sun filtered through a sparse canopy of leafy trees. Planting a sun-lover in the dense shade of a hemlock or spruce tree isn't a good plan if you want it to bloom.

Morning sun is less powerful than afternoon sun. If you want to grow a shade-loving plant in a sunny spot, plant it where it only gets morning sun. The same number of hours of afternoon sun might be fatal or at least cause its leaves to discolor. Most shade plants will survive better in sunny spots if they have consistently moist soil, not dry soil.

Soil type: You can adjust soil conditions to suit most plants. The majority of perennials want pretty much the same thing: rich, dark soil full of organic matter that stays lightly moist but is not soggy. If your soil doesn't fit the bill, add compost or old manure—two or three shovels of compost worked into the site for the new perennial. And don't be lazy: Loosen and improve the soil in a 2-foot-diameter circle for a perennial; don't just dig a hole big enough to squeeze in the root ball. Each time I plant a perennial I add half a cup of organic fertilizer and half a cup each of greensand, rock phosphate, and rock powder and stir it in well.

If you want a lean soil, meaning one without much nitrogen, don't add fertilizer.

Perennial Flowers and Bulbs

How Big a Hole Should I Dig?

When planting a perennial, don't just dig a hole the size of the pot. That's like buying snug sneakers for a teenager. For a perennial in a one-gallon pot (7 inches wide and 8 inches deep), loosen up and improve the soil in a 2-foot-diameter circle and about 1 foot deep. If you are planting something that will get huge, say a clump of phlox, prepare a wider hole. And for plants with deep roots like peonies, dig deeper.

If a plant needs sandy soil, dig a hole and take away some of the soil. Bring in sand and mix it with compost, two shovels of compost for every one of sand, then stir it in with the soil from the hole.

Soil pH: The vast majority of perennials like a slightly acidic soil, in the range of pH 6.0 to 6.8. Soil in the woods or fields of Vermont varies considerably, so you'll probably want to test your garden's pH before planting much.

If your soil test reveals a pH below 6, you can add limestone or wood ashes, as explained in chapter 1. If the pH is above 7, you can make your soil more acidic by adding elemental sulfur (approved for use by organic gardeners) or by using an organic fertilizer such as Pro-Holly or Holly-Tone. All of those soil additives take time—often months—to change the pH. And follow the directions. More is not better.

Soil moisture: Adding compost and organic matter will improve soil's ability to process water. If you are planting a dozen perennials in a new flower bed, it doesn't make sense to improve the soil only in the holes where you intend to put each plant. Add a layer of compost 4 to 6 inches thick to the entire bed and work it in all over. That will really do something good for your soil: improving soil tilth and structure, helping your soil drain better in wet times, and holding water in hot, dry months.

How to Grow Moisture-Loving Plants on a Dry Hillside

A large plastic bag buried deep beneath a perennial will help retain water and can make a big difference in a plant's performance. I planted two moisture-loving plants, astilbes, side by side on a dry hillside; in each case I added compost and the minerals I normally use. But for one, I also "planted" a black plastic bag about a foot beneath the surface and poked a few holes in it with my pocketknife. The astilbe planted over the bag has become a bigger, more impressive plant.

Soil temperature: You might not think you can do much about Vermont's cold winters, but you can. If you have a plant that is marginally hardy for your zone, wait until the ground freezes, then mulch it with wood chips or leaves. This will accomplish two things: It will minimize freezing and thawing, which can push plants up (especially first-year plants) and expose their roots to air; and it will act as a blanket against extreme cold.

Fortunately most years Vermont has a good, thick layer of snow on the ground for the coldest parts of winter, which acts as a blanket, protecting roots. Cold can travel sideways, too, so don't plant tender perennials near the edge of a terrace.

The Classics

Here is a list of my favorite perennials. Every Vermont garden should have most of these, if not all. They are easy to grow, beautiful, and nearly foolproof. There are many other wonderful plants, but these have withstood the test of time, and most are hardy throughout Vermont—from the Canadian border to the

Staking

Many tall perennials, and some annuals, will flop if left to their own devices. They will be healthier and look better with some help from you. Buy a package of 4-foot bamboo stakes at the garden center. Things like hollyhocks and delphinium will probably need 6-foot stakes. You can always snip off stakes if they are too tall.

For a single spike, push the stake 6-inches or so into the ground behind the flower spike. I use green plastic staking material that comes in a roll, but string can be used or paper-covered wire that is also sold at garden centers. I attach the tie material to the stake with a clove hitch—or any knot that will not slip. I leave both ends long, encircle the plant, and tie the ends together with a simple square knot. Stakes can also be used to make a supporting "fence." Push them in at a 45 degree angle, crisscrossing each other. Large plants can lean against the stakes, staying upright.

Massachusetts line. A few are marked hardy only to Zone 4, but they would probably survive even in the coldest spots in the state if the soil conditions were right. These beauties are listed in the order they bloom in my garden.

Primroses (*Primula* spp.): There are many species of primroses, most of which bloom in spring or early summer. In general they like moist, rich soil in filtered shade or morning sun. They do especially well under old apple trees. My favorite is a relatively unknown one with no common name, *P. kisoana*; it has pinky magenta blossoms, and for me it spreads fast by root in either moist or dry soil, but doesn't force others out of its way. Its fuzzy leaves make a great ground cover, too.

Another great one is the candelabra primrose (*P. japonica*), which blooms in June, displaying tiers of flowers on bare stems 18 to 24 inches above the leaves. These spread well by seed for me without any help.

Bleeding heart (*Dicentra spectabilis*): Given rich, slightly moist soil and half a day of sun or more, this beauty will grow to 3 feet tall and wide in a few years. It has long sprays of small deep pink and white blossoms; it blooms for three to four weeks. The leaves tend to yellow and die by August in dry soils or hot, sunny locations, but they stay looking good later in moist soil or locations with morning sun only. They have deep fleshy taproots and do not transplant easily, but they often self-sow and the small seedlings move easily. Bleeding heart comes in a pure white form, *D. alba* ("alba" means white in Latin).

Peonies (*Paeonia* spp.): These are dramatic, wonderful flowers—many with scents so lovely as to nearly make one swoon. They are not without problems, however: Many peonies have double flowers, meaning that they have many layers of petals, which makes them prone to flopping after a rain. You need to stake these plants or buy peony cages to surround them. There are single varieties, with just one set of petals, and these rarely flop.

Peonies will live forever, almost, if planted well. They have deep taproots, so planting even a small one means digging a hole 2 feet deep and 2 feet across and filling it with rich soil, compost, minerals, and fertilizer. They need sweet soil, so mix a cup of ground limestone or wood ashes into the soil at planting time. The eye of the tuber needs to be within an inch of the soil surface, or the peony won't bloom.

Siberian iris (*Iris siberica*): These bloom at about the same time as peonies, and the two make a wonderful combination. Iris blossoms are short lived but come in deep, rich blues and purples that are almost heart-stoppingly beautiful. They need to be divided every five years or so because they use up the soil nutrients and gradually the center of a clump dies out. Top-dressing early in spring with organic fertilizer (that is, sprinkling some fertilizer on top of the clump) helps to minimize this.

Black-eyed Susans: All members of the genus *Rudbeckia* are easy to grow and beautiful. My favorite is 'Prairie Sun' (*Rudbeckia hirta*). A relatively new introduction, this is a named cultivar with a green eye that blooms profusely for me from mid-July until Halloween. An excellent cut flower, it forms nice clumps with flower stems 18 to 24 inches tall.

Delphinium (*Delphinium* spp.): These are spectacular flowers. Some of the bigger ones (Pacific hybrids, for example) send up flower stalks 5 feet tall (or more) in rich blues and purples. But like peonies they must be staked, and even then they sometimes break in rainstorms. They need fertile soil in full sun. Shorter varieties such as 'Blue Butterfly', which is less than 2 feet tall, rarely flop. *D. chinensis* is also short with delicate, fernlike foliage, but is less hardy than some other species. To minimize flopping and encourage reblooming, cut stems of delphinium right to the ground after blooming. Top-dress with organic fertilizer each spring.

Lilies (*Lilium* spp.): Oriental lilies are fragrant, big, and brassy. The Asiatics are unscented and a little more delicate. These beauties, both the Orientals and the Asiatics, are in trouble. The lily leaf beetle has devastated lilies in southern Vermont, and the beetles are moving north. Handpicking helps, but it may not be enough to keep the beetles under control. If need be, I am willing to give up on lilies until a biological control is available. (See chapter 12 for more information about combating these pests.)

My substitute for lilies has been an annual flower called Angel's Trumpet (*Datura* spp.). This has the big flowers of Oriental lilies and produces blossoms much of the summer. It likes full to part sun and rich moist soil. It is available in white or purple; I find the white ones more vigorous. The seeds are poisonous if eaten.

Daylilies (*Hemerocallis* spp.): Daylilies are indestructible and will grow just about anywhere. Dump a clump of orange daylilies on your lawn? Next year it will be a handsome plant. Not true lilies, they are not affected by the lily leaf beetle, either. They prefer full sun and good soil but will grow anywhere.

There are fanatics out there breeding and hybridizing daylilies, so you'll find thousands of named cultivars. The best-known variety is the old-fashioned foundation lily, a bright orange. But daylilies come in various pastels, some with dark eyes, others with ruffled edges. Some are early bloomers, some bloom late into the fall. Some flower scapes (leafless stems) are under 1 foot high, most are 18 to 30 inches, and a few reach 6 feet.

Perennial bachelor buttons (*Centaurea montana*): Spidery blue 2-inch blossoms on 18-inch stems appear in early summer, but if you cut them back—or pick the blossoms for vases—the plants might rebloom for you. And they may self-seed, appearing where you didn't plant them. It's a fairly drought-tolerant plant.

Foxglove (*Digitalis* spp.): The most common foxglove, *D. purpurea*, is not a perennial at all, even though it is often sold as such. It's a biennial, a flower that gets established its first year of life, then blooms, sets seed, and dies in its second year. The flower stems are lined with small pink and purple blossoms that bloom on stalks from 18 to 36 inches tall. When the tiny seeds are black and ripe, cut a stem and shake it over an area where you'd like plants in two years. I do this along the edges of woods or fields. Foxgloves have so many seeds that a few grow even though I don't prepare the soil.

There is one cultivar, 'Foxy', that will bloom the first year if started indoors early, which is nice for Zone 3 gardeners, as foxglove is a Zone 4 plant. There are perennial foxgloves such as *D.*

lutea, a smaller, delicate brown-freckled yellow, that is a perennial even in Zone 3 and a bigger version, called *D. grandifolia*, also yellow, that is also perennial.

Catmint (*Nepeta x faassenii*): Related to catnip, this is a hybrid plant with silvery gray mounding foliage and small trumpet-shaped blue flowers. 'Six Hills Giant' is one of the best cultivars. Cut catmint back after flowering and it may rebloom.

Pink mallow (*Malva alcea*): I know that "serious" gardeners, the ones who only use Latin names, will laugh at me for this choice and call it a thug. It's a generous plant: big, blowsy, pink, and beautiful; some might even call it slatternly. Plenty of blossoms, plenty of babies. I love it for its midsummer cheeriness. It has a fleshy taproot and doesn't transplant well. Get a tiny one from a friend in early spring—we all have it. Deadhead it regularly to keep it blooming and to minimize volunteer seedlings; shear it back by a third in early June for smaller plant size and less flopping.

Bee balm (*Monarda didyma*): Bee balm is big (3 to 4 feet) and beautiful, fragrant (minty), colorful (mainly in shades of red and purple), and a great cut flower. It likes full sun, but mine flourish with morning sun and good soil. It doesn't thrive in hot, dry locations. It blooms in midsummer, a time when many gardens need blooms.

Its flaw? It spreads by root and can quickly overwhelm a flower bed when you turn your back on it for ten minutes. Or a season or two. But it pulls up easily, so I don't consider it a thug. I've tried containing it with plastic edging, but still it wandered. It can get covered with unsightly mildew, but newer varieties have been bred to minimize that.

Shasta daisies (*Leucanthemum x superbum*): This white daisy is a great cut flower and a cheery addition to any garden. It is a short-lived perennial unless you divide it every two or three years, in which case it stays vigorous. It needs full sun and doesn't want to spend the winter in a soggy soil.

Sneezeweed (*Helenium autumnale*): This great fall flower offers clusters of small daisy-like flowers on tall stems in interesting colors: mahogany and red and yellow, sometimes all three on each blossom. There's a pure yellow one; others have dark red as the dominant color. It likes full sun and tolerates moist soils. It is hardy to Zone 4.

FYI: Sneezeweed is not a big allergy producer. I've read that it got its common name from the fact that back in days of taking snuff, it was sometimes ground and inhaled to stimulate sneezing.

Lesser-Known Perennials for the Woodland

Sarah and Gary Milek run Cider Hill Gardens (www.ciderhillgardens .com) in Windsor, where they have an incredible collection of unusual perennials and cultivated wildflowers on display and for sale. They specialize in interesting woodland plants and in Gary's paintings and prints, which feature woodland scenes or plants from their peony, daylily, and hosta collections. Here are some of their suggested plants for shady places or a woodland garden. Their soil is about pH neutral. If you live in a part of Vermont with acid soils, you will need to add limestone at planting time. Most of the following plants are not commonly found in ordinary garden centers—or in most plant books, either.

Doll's-eyes (*Actea pachypoda*): A native wildflower, this has creamy white delicate flowers in spring. Its true value, however, is for the berries in fall: white, with dark "eyes." Red baneberry (*A. rubra*) is similar, but with red berries. Both Actea like moist, dappled shade and grow to be 20 to 30 inches tall on stiff stems. Zone 3.

Great Solomon's seal (*Polygonatum canaliculatum*): Stems 3 or 4 feet long or more display small white tubular flowers hanging down in rows along the stems in early summer. The handsome foliage persists all summer. It does well in shade to dappled shade. Zone 3.

Greek valerian (*Polemonium reptans*): This low-growing (12 inches) perennial that spreads by root is related to the common Jacob's ladder. It has purple to lavender ½-inch-diameter flowers. It naturalizes nicely but doesn't take over. It does best in moist woods but tolerates dry shade to part sun. Zone 4.

Shooting stars (*Dodecatheon* spp.): These bloom in May or June, then disappear in summer. Their white, pink, or lavender flowers, on naked stems 6 to 12 inches tall, look like tiny umbrellas blown inside out. They need rich, moist soil in light shade. Zone 4.

Spikenard (*Aralia racemosa*): Large compound leaves grow on stems up to 48 inches long, which terminate in narrow panicles of greenish-white fluffy flowers in mid-July. In fall spikenard displays attractive blue berries smaller than peas. It does best in shade to light shade with rich, slightly moist soil. This is a very handsome plant all summer. Zone 4.

Virginia bluebells (*Mertensia virginica*): These native beauties start out early in spring with pinkish buds that turn to blue as they open. Lovely bell-shaped flowers open in sequence over a period of three weeks. They need moist, sunny conditions in spring and shade in summer. They are ephemerals, meaning the foliage disappears soon after plants finish blooming. Despite the name Virginia, this bluebell is hardy to Zone 3 and naturalizes nicely when happy.

My own pick for a woodland perennial? The pink lady's slipper, *Cypripedium acaule*. A wildflower that is impossible to move, I've never grown one. But every time I come across one in the woods, my heart nearly stops. Scott Durkee of New Haven, Vermont, has developed a way to propagate lady's slippers in the laboratory, and he now sells them through his website, www.vtladyslipper.com. In the wild pink lady's slippers grow in pockets of humus in areas dominated by pine, hemlock, spruce, oak, or beech trees. They need well-drained soil with a pH of 3.5 to 4.5, which is very acidic. Some morning sun is ideal.

Shade Perennials

Shade perennials, in general, are more understated than the flashy full-sun flowers. Primroses, a shade plant discussed in "The Classics," are dramatic, and astilbes can be, too.

Astilbe (*Astilbe* spp.): These shade perennials do best with rich, moist soil; they also grow in sun if plenty of moisture is present. Bushy, airy flower spikes of tiny blossoms come in shades of red, pink, and white. They are excellent cut flowers with strong stems, so grow plenty.

European wild ginger (*Asarum europaeum*): This is grown for its glossy round leaves, each 2 to 3 inches in diameter. It likes rich soil and tolerates dry soil. As a ground cover, it can shade out most weeds.

Hostas (*Hosta* spp.): Every garden center will have plenty of these, the backbone of shade gardens. Their leaves come in all sizes from tiny to huge and in colors from blue green to lime green. Learn to appreciate the leaves, as generally the flowers are not dramatic.

Lungwort (*Pulmonaria* spp.): This is a very early bloomer with spotted leaves that look good all summer long and into the fall when other plants have browned and died back. The small blossoms come in blue, red, white, and peach—and sometimes more than one color blossom on the same plant. Spreads by root.

Sweet woodruff (*Galium odoratum*): This lesser-known gem has leaves arranged in whorls around the stem and dainty white, fragrant flowers in June. It spreads nicely by root in moist soils; in dry soils the foliage may die out in August. An excellent ground cover.

Wild (or fringed) bleeding heart (*Dicentra exemia*): Sold in all nurseries, it isn't really wild anymore. It is one of the few perennials that will bloom most of the summer if the soil stays moist. It has small pink to purple or white heart-shaped flowers.

Fragrant Perennial Herbs

Sarah and Gary Milek of Cider Hill Gardens cultivate a wide range of scented flowers and herbs. Here are some of Sarah's favorites.

Artemisias: This is a large group of plants with fragrant flowers and leaves. Sarah grows one of my favorites: *A. lactiflora*. Also known as white mugwort, it forms nice clumps and has fine-leafed foliage with tiny, milky white flowers in mid- to late summer. *A. dracunculus* is the tarragon used in the kitchen. Be sure to ask for French tarragon if you want to cook with it. *A. camphorata* is Sarah's choice for powerful fragrance. A patented variety of wormwood artemesia called 'Oriental Limelight' has handsome yellow and green variegated leaves. Most artemisias are hardy to Zone 4.

Lavender (*Lavandula* spp.): The scent of foliage and the spikes of lavender blue flowers make this a highly desirable plant. The cultivar 'Munstead' is reliably hardy in Zone 4, while others survive only to Zone 5. The Mileks grow lavender in well-drained, almost gravely soil and mulch it with marble chips. It needs sweet soil, pH 7 or above. Me? I grow it in pots so I can control the soil conditions more easily and bring it in for the winter. Even then I sometimes lose it during the winter.

Lemon balm (*Melissa officinalis*): Great for use as a tea, lemon balm is related to bee balm, but unlike bee balm (*Monarda*) it doesn't spread by root to take over the garden— though lemon balm will self-sow and spread if happy. Bees of all sort love this plant. Zone 4.

Mountain mint (*Pycanthemum virginianum*): Not related to standard invasive mints (*Menthus* spp.), mountain mint has attractive finely cut leaves and clusters of tiny white flowers. I use the leaves for tea. Grow it in full sun in moist soil or semi- shaded in drier soils. Zone 4.

Oregano (*Origanum vulgare*): Greek oregano is the best-tasting variety, so ask for it when buying oregano for culinary uses. Oregano grows to be 18 inches tall but tends to flop. It does best in full sun with well-drained soil. Zone 4.

Salvia (*Salvia* spp.): Common salvia (*S. officinalis*) is the sage we use in the kitchen, but there are some 900 species in this genus, many of which have fragrant leaves or flowers. The Mileks grow several sages in their Zone 4 garden, although many books list sage as a Zone 5 perennial. It features lovely blue flowers.

Thyme (*Thymus* spp.): Like the artemisias, there are plenty of thymes, many of which can be used as fragrant ground covers. Sarah loves the golden lime-green leaves of *T. praecox* 'Golden', which she uses as a ground cover. Lemon thyme (*T. x citriodorus*) is vigorous and fragrant. Thymes do best in hot, dry locations, so Sarah mulches hers with small marble chips or turkey grit, available at feed stores. Good drainage is also key. Zone 4.

Wildflowers

Vermont is rich in wildflowers, and I can't discuss them all here. But here are three great ones that are often available in garden centers. The New England Wild Flower Society (see chapter 14) also sells hundreds of kinds of wildflowers at the Garden in the Woods, in Framingham, Massachusetts. Go in spring for a visual treat.

Please do not dig up wildflowers from the woods and bring them home. You'll most likely fail—most don't transplant well. And you may adversely affect their population in the woods.

Bloodroot (*Sanguinaria canadensis*): Bloodroot's green leaves emerge very early in spring, rolled up like cigars, opening to round leaves 5 to 8 inches in diameter. The white flowers last just a few days, but for me they are true harbingers of spring. Doubles, though frightfully expensive, look like miniature white roses, and they bloom longer than the singles. Bloodroot leaves stay nice all summer if the plant is grown in slightly moist light shade. Zone 3.

Jack-in-the-pulpit (*Arisaema triphyllum*): Not only is the strange-looking flower (a dark figure—Jack—sheathed in a green curled leafy arrangement) interesting in spring, it shows off with red berries in late summer. It does best in rich, moist soil and medium shade, though I also have it in dry soil—it's just not as vigorous. Zone 4.

Trillium (*Trillium* spp.): Another great genus of wildflowers everyone should grow. Trilliums have three leaves on a solitary stem and deep purple or white three-petaled flowers above the leaves. Trillium blooms in early spring and prefers moist, well-drained soils. Most species are hardy to Zone 3.

Lesser-Known Bulb Plants

Everyone knows the standard flowering bulbs: crocuses, daffodils, hyacinths, and tulips. They're great plants, but there are also bulb plants that are equally good but not so common—and some bloom in autumn.

Most bulbs need well-drained soil. Early spring bloomers can be planted under deciduous trees—the bulbs get their sunshine to charge them up for another season before the tree leaves shade them. Here are some of my spring-to-fall favorites (all are hardy to Zone 3 unless otherwise noted).

Snowdrops (*Galanthus nivalis*): These guys must have kerosene in their veins, as they are undaunted by cold and literally push up through frozen soil every year. Their tiny white blossoms are best shown off in large numbers, so start with fifty bulbs if you can. Divide after blooming every few years; they multiply nicely.

Winter aconite (*Eranthis hyemalis*): Bright yellow, these are almost as early as snowdrops. They have buttercup-like flowers that hug the ground. Hardy to Zone 4.

Scilla (*Scilla siberica*): These small, intensely purple flowers are early bloomers, following and overlapping with snowdrops, time-wise. Many are needed for a good show.

Glory-of-the-snow (*Chionodoxa luciliae*): These are also early bloomers, appearing with scilla. They have vivid blue flowers with light-colored centers. I like these better than scilla because they look up, showing their faces, while scilla look downward.

Grape hyacinth (*Muscari* spp.): These cuties look vaguely like 2-inch cluster of grapes upside down on 3-inch stems. They bloom mid-spring and come in blues, purples, whites, and bicolors. Unlike most other bulbs, they send up a few leaves in the fall. I use them as markers—I plant some with my daffodils or tulips to mark any locations where I shouldn't dig when planting bulbs in the fall.

Allium spp.: These are wonderful relatives of the onions and chives you already know. My favorites include the drumstick allium (*A. sphaerocephalon*), which has 1- to 2-inch clusters of reddish purple blossoms at the tips of thin, wiry stems 18 to 24 inches long. Great cut flowers, and, if dried, will look good for a year in an arrangement.

Then there is *A. giganteum* (hardy to Zone 4), which has a stem 3 to 4 feet tall with a globe of florets 5 to 6 inches in diameter. Truly spectacular. The seedpods look good long after the bloom. Star-of-Persia (*A. christophii*) has even bigger blossoms, reminiscent of fireworks. Most alliums bloom early to midsummer. Both are hardy to Zone 4, and are not be eaten by rodents

If you grow leeks in the vegetable garden, let a few winter over: They will bloom magnificently their second year, though then you can't eat the leek. All alliums are wonderful.

Colchicum (*Colchicum autumnale*): These gems look like crocuses on steroids. The bulbs are large and should be planted in late summer or early fall. They come as singles or doubles and in pinky-lavender or white. They surprise me every fall as they pop out of the ground without the accompaniment of leaves. The leaves appear in spring, then disappear.

Each bulb may send up half a dozen blossoms in sequence; their only failing is that they flop. Plant a ground cover like sweet woodruff or vinca around colchicums to help prop up their blossoms. They bloom late in the season, and I use them as cut flowers when there are no others left in the garden to grace the table.

Fall crocus (*Crocus sativus, C. speciosus*): These crocuses are very late, sometimes blooming until Thanksgiving, and often producing more than one blossom per bulb. Less hardy than spring crocuses, some will die off in hard winters in Zone 4, but all should be good for Zone 5. Plant in fall for fall bloom.

Putting the Garden to Bed

Each fall I spend many hours putting my garden to bed. I use a serrated knife to slice through flower stems a handful at a time. I pull weeds as I go; it's surprising how many have snuck in and hidden themselves among the tall plants. By ridding the garden of weeds in the fall, I save myself work in the spring. Weeds and grasses generally wake up and start growing before garden flowers, so they can easily take over a bed before you are ready to start gardening in spring.

I don't cut down everything, though. I leave a few tall plants with stiff stems that I can see from our kitchen window. Snug inside, I enjoy seeing them nodding to me above the snow or dancing in winter winds.

Final Thoughts

Just for fun, try this: Ask your gardening friends and neighbors what their favorite perennial flower is. Most will demure, saying it's impossible to choose just one, no more than anyone would be willing to single out one child as best. So ask for several picks. If a friend really loves something, and you don't know it or grow it, give it a try!

Perennials are amazing in their diversity of size, color, form, and fragrance. But if I had to grow just one? It would be the peony 'Festiva Maxima'. It is a double white with a drop of red in the center and a fragrance so sweet and intense that I've often wondered why no one has made a perfume of it. 'Festiva Maxima' only blooms for a week or two, and a heavy rain will knock stems to the ground. But if I were marooned on an island, I would want this plant.

CHAPTER EIGHT

Trees and Shrubs

It may seem to you by March that Vermont's winter lasts forever. That the old joke is true: Vermont has just two seasons, winter and the Fourth of July. Because growing flowers and vegetables is limited by the cold, it's important to grow trees and shrubs that have grace and beauty all year round. We need woody plants that stand up above the snow. Trees with handsome bark and form or with berries that will feed the birds and please you as you look out the window on a blustery winter day.

This chapter discusses how to plant and prune trees and shrubs, and provides information about many of the trees and shrubs that do well in Vermont—from the classic shrubs that thrive anywhere to some lesser-known greats; from native trees important for birds to handsome street trees for urban use.

How to Plant Trees

Planting a tree involves much more than just digging a big hole and plunking in a sapling. Planted too deeply, most trees will never make it to maturity or will limp along and never reach their potential. Bark—resistant to rot aboveground—will rot underground. A deeply planted tree will slowly decline until, by age ten or fifteen, it is ready for the woodpile. Here's the proper way to plant any tree.

First, Find the Trunk Flare

Your mission, before you dig a hole, is to find the trunk flare of your young tree and then make sure it's aboveground once planted. Look at trees growing in the forest. Notice how the trunk flares out and "roots" appear to snake across the ground a little before disappearing beneath the surface. That flare must be above ground to grow a healthy tree.

Commercial growers plant trees like corn, close together in rows. When the trees reach a certain size, the trees are pulled up (without soil); some are slapped into a pot right away, and others are shipped first. In either case the pot is filled with soil and often the trunk flare is buried. Take a good look at the tree you're about to plant. Can you see the trunk flare? If not, you need to remove soil from the surface until you find it. Take your time. The flare may be covered by 3 to 6 inches of soil in the pot, depending on the size of the pot.

Small fibrous roots may have started growing above the trunk flare if it's been buried in soil for a year or more at the nursery. Ignore or trim off those rootlets. Keep looking for the point at which the trunk flares out. It is not always easy, especially for very small trees. Also look for roots that have hit the side of the plastic pot and are circling around the trunk. They need to be teased out at planting time or they can choke other roots and cause parts of your tree to die.

Digging the Hole

Having found the trunk flare, measure the distance from it to the bottom of the pot. That's how deep your hole should be, no deeper. That means your tree will be sitting on unexcavated soil—so it won't settle later—and the flare will be visible.

It's always better to plant a tree in a hole that is a little shallow rather than in a hole that is too deep. For large trees, some experts prefer to feel around for the trunk flare, but they don't remove all the soil covering it at planting time. Instead, they advise you to let it get settled in for a year, then remove the excess soil that is covering the trunk flare the second year. But don't forget to do this!

A planting hole should have gently sloping sides and be three to four times as wide as the root ball. Why so wide? Even after you backfill the hole, the soil will be looser than the soil in surrounding areas, allowing fine roots to penetrate it more easily.

Normally you shouldn't add compost or fertilizer to the soil when you backfill the hole. You don't want to create a bathtub of good soil that encourages roots to stay put, enjoying a life of luxury, as it were. You want them to extend far and wide, and they will have to get used to the soil you have.

In cases of extremely poor soil, dig a much wider hole and mix the crummy soil half and half with good garden soil—even if you have to buy it. But be sure to choose a tree that can survive in poor soils if that's what you have. Ask for a good street tree at the nursery if you have poor soil.

What can you do to help the tree get established? For a good-sized tree, sprinkle a one-pound coffee can full of rock or colloidal

When to Plant a Tree

There are two schools of thought on this. I prefer planting trees in the fall, as it's cooler and generally we have more rain. Roots continue to grow even after leaf drop, and without leaves to lose moisture there is less chance of dehydration—a major cause of death in young trees. But be sure to plant at least a month before the ground freezes, and then apply a 4-inch thick layer of mulch around the planting zone to keep the soil warm late into the fall.

The other school of thought is that our winters are harsh, so we should let trees get established all summer before they face the cold. This requires that you water your new tree once a week all summer long. Don't keep the soil saturated, but don't let it dry out. If you can do that, planting in spring is fine.

phosphate in the bottom of the hole, and scratch it in (use less for small trees). Mix in another can of the same into the backfill. Rock phosphate doesn't move through soil easily, and it promotes good root growth. Greensand, Azomite, or rock powders are good to add, too, as described in chapter 1.

Planting

Before planting, it is a good idea to soak the pot or root ball in a bucket of water to get the roots soaked. As you backfill the hole, carefully pack the soil around the root ball with your hands or tamp it with the handle of your spade. You want to eliminate any air pockets. Create a raised lip of soil at the edge of your planting to hold in water. That way water won't run off and will soak down deep. Water once or twice a week. A sprinkler mimics rain, which is good; put out a tuna can to see how long it takes the sprinkler to deliver an inch of rain, the amount you should provide with each watering. If using a sprinkler isn't practical, use a bucket and provide five gallons each time for a large tree. Young trees need some watering their second year, too, particularly if Vermont has a hot, dry summer.

Cover the planting zone with 2 to 3 inches of bark mulch, but keep the mulch away from the trunk. You don't want to cover the trunk flare with mulch, as it will cause bark rot. Mulch volcanoes, though common, can be deadly.

Before I knew better, I planted an apple tree in a deep hole full of manure and garden soil. I covered the trunk flare. The roots stayed in the bathtub I'd created. The trunk rotted. I never got more than a couple of apples from that tree, and I yanked it out after ten years. Don't make my mistakes!

Taking Care of the Newly Planted Tree

Once planted, trees really need very little care. Mother Nature doesn't supply fertilizer spikes or spray pesticides, and you don't need to, either. There are two things you can do that will vastly improve the chances of a newly planted tree surviving: Water it regularly, and protect it from weed whackers (string trimmers). To keep the weed whackers away from your tree, mulch around it so there will be no grass or weeds nearby, or plant a ground cover that need not be mowed. If the bark gets sliced through by a string trimmer or lawn mower, nutrients and water are cut off to a portion of the tree. If the tree is girdled, it will die. No second chance.

Pruning Deciduous Trees and Shrubs

Most people look forward to pruning their trees and shrubs about as much as they look forward to preparing their taxes. As a result, many planted trees and (especially) shrubs are formless, messy, and cluttered. I love to prune. It is an opportunity to create sculpture, but without the tedious chipping away of granite or wood with a chisel. I think most people don't prune because they don't know just what to do, and they are afraid of doing something awful, something irreversible to their precious tree or shrub. Better to leave it till next year than make a mistake now, many think. The trouble is that "next year" never comes.

March is the best time to prune fruit trees. Evergreens should be pruned in early summer, just after they have put on their new growth. Fall is a good time to prune deciduous trees and shrubs (those that that lose their leaves). Once they have lost their leaves, it is easy to see their form—and their problems. Insects and diseases are dormant and less likely to attack an open wound in fall.

A word or two first about tools to use: The technology has changed in the past twenty years, so you should think about getting some new tools. Sharp is important. That rusty old-fashioned bow saw you've had hanging in the garage for years is not what you want.

Pruning saws now have tricut blades with teeth so sharp that they go through hardwood like the proverbial hot knife through butter. This is good: A sharp saw gives a clean cut and doesn't tear.

The new saws can't be sharpened, or not by most of us, but they are worth the price and will last for years if you keep them clean and don't misuse them by cutting roots. Bypass pruning shears and loppers are also needed.

Before you begin pruning, it is important to know where to make your cuts. Although trees vary considerably in the shape of their branches, most have a swollen area called the branch collar where the branch meets the trunk or a larger branch. Often you will see wrinkled bark at the outer edge of the branch collar. It is important not to cut into the collar but to prune just beyond it (away from the trunk or larger branch).

The collar produces chemicals against invading disease. A flush cut tight to the trunk removes the collar and opens up a large area to disease. In the 1950s we were told to make flush cuts and to paint them with tar. Now research indicates that these are not good practices.

If you are cutting a large branch, you need to make three cuts to remove the branch without risk of tearing the bark and damaging the collar. Remove most of the weight of the branch by making two quick cuts: First, make an undercut about one-third of the way through the branch to be removed—about 12 inches from the branch collar. This will prevent a tear from extending into the collar. Then, a little farther out the branch (away from the trunk), make a top cut that will sever the branch. Finally make a cut at the edge of the branch collar, removing the stub that you just created. Because the stub is lightweight, there is little danger of tearing, especially if you can support it with one hand.

Now you are ready for surgery. Stand back and look at the tree or shrub. Is the form pleasing to you? Do you see strong lines? Is it the shape you hoped for when you bought it? Keep these thoughts in mind as you get to work.

The first step is to remove all deadwood. This might seem tricky in fall or winter without leaves to guide you, but it isn't. Dead branches are brittle, their color is different, and their bark may be flaking off. If you scrape the bark on a branch with your fingernail, a live branch will show green; a dead branch will not. You can remove deadwood anytime of the year.

Next look for branches that are crossing or rubbing, and prune out the smaller or least desirable branch. If the branches have fused, you may decide to eliminate them both.

Then look for branches that are damaged, cracked, or in poor health. A tree in good condition shouldn't have too many of these. Cut them back to healthy wood or remove the branch entirely.

Fourth, look at branches that are competing for the same sunlight. Sometimes two branches will grow parallel to each other. One will shade out the other, so remove one, leaving the stronger, fuller branch.

Fifth, eliminate the "invaders." These are branches that spot an opportunity to catch some sunlight and reach out for it like a teenager going for the last cookie on the plate. Invaders ignore the basic branching patterns and clutter up the interior of your tree or shrub. Often they become rubbing or crossing branches.

Lastly, prune out water sprouts. These are small branches that tend to shoot straight up from larger branches. They are often an indication of a tree in stress, a tree's way of producing extra leaves and thus additional capacity to make food.

Many fruit trees produce numerous water sprouts every year, in part as a response to heavy pruning done previously. In the heat of the summer, the leaves at the top of the tree become dormant due to the heat. The interior part of the tree is cooler and remains better able to produce food. Instead of eliminating all of the water sprouts, try training a few to fill in the interior of the tree. This should slow down the annual production of water sprouts.

For years I followed the pruning rule that it was all right to remove up to one-third of a tree if necessary. Current thinking is that it is better to remove no more than 15 to 20 percent of the live branches on any given year. Cutting off branches may make your tree look better, but you are also reducing its ability to produce

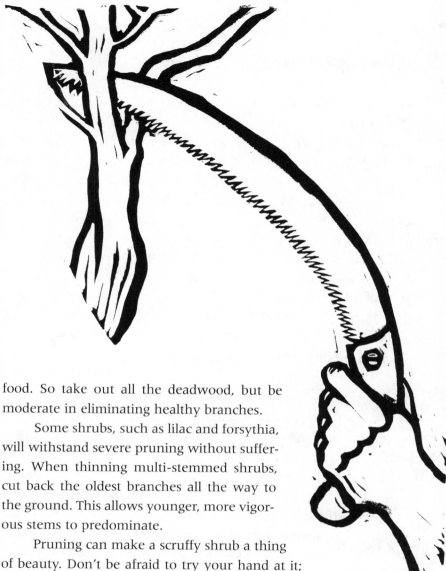

food. So take out all the deadwood, but be moderate in eliminating healthy branches.

Some shrubs, such as lilac and forsythia, will withstand severe pruning without suffering. When thinning multi-stemmed shrubs, cut back the oldest branches all the way to the ground. This allows younger, more vigorous stems to predominate.

Pruning can make a scruffy shrub a thing of beauty. Don't be afraid to try your hand at it; almost anything you do is fixable. Trees and shrubs will respond to pruning by becoming healthier and more vigorous. If you take off a branch in an "oops!" moment, another will eventually take its place. Take your time, especially at first, and step back often to look at the entire plant. You will be rewarded not only with a more handsome plant but also a better appreciation for its form, texture, and personality.

Pruning Evergreens

Pruning evergreens is done largely to keep trees and shrubs from getting too big. Blue spruces, for example, are sometimes purchased when small and cute. People are shocked to find them blocking their windows and reaching skyward just a few years later.

Pines, spruce, and hemlocks don't get cluttered up with water sprouts or invaders. Their branches grow in nice neat rows off the main trunk.

To keep an evergreen small, prune off each year's new growth when you can still see the difference in color between new and old growth. Generally that is in June. It is very difficult to keep a tree small if it is genetically destined to be 60 feet. If you want a small evergreen, get a dwarf cultivar, or one that grows very, very slowly.

Good Trees for Vermont

Vermont is home to dozens of species of wonderful trees. You probably know the sugar maple, white birch, white pine, and Canadian hemlock. But many other species of trees are hardy here, including some uncommon ones that you may wish to see and eventually to plant.

Dr. Norman Pellett is a retired professor of horticulture, formerly with the University of Vermont. He has authored two books useful to Vermonters interested in planting trees: *Landscape Plants for Vermont*, written with Dr. Mark Starrett, associate professor at UVM, and *Native Shrubs and Vines for Northern New England Landscapes* (see chapter 14). We toured the Horticulture Farm in South Burlington and looked at some of Pellett's favorites trees, which include the following:

Amur maackia (*Maackia amurensis*): A good medium-sized street tree that will survive poor soil and dry conditions, it grows only 20 to 25 feet tall and about 15 feet wide. Spikes of pealike white flowers appear in late June or early July. It has attractive bark and an overall form that is pleasantly rounded. Grow it in sun. Zone 4.

Korean mountain ash (*Sorbus alnifolia*): This tree offers white flowers in late May, gorgeous small red fruit in the fall, and fine-textured foliage. Trees reach 25 to 40 feet tall and 25 to 35 feet wide. Zone 4.

Sargent cherry (*Prunus sargentii*): Profuse pink flowers in early to mid-May are followed by dark fruit in late June on an upright, oval tree. Attractive dark reddish bark and excellent fall leaf color. It prefers full sun and grows to 25 to 40 feet tall at maturity. Zone 4.

Silver linden (*Tilia tomentosa*): Leaves are green on top but white and fuzzy underneath, giving this linden a silvery color in the wind. It is planted as a street tree in parts of Burlington. Bearing small fragrant flowers in June, it grows 50 to 70 feet tall by 40 to 50 feet wide in full sun. Zone 4.

Snowberry mountain ash (*Sorbus discolor*): Similar to the Korean mountain ash, but smaller at 20 to 25 feet tall and 12 to 20 feet wide, the snowberry mountain ash bears pink or yellowish fruit in fall. It prefers good drainage and full sun. Zone 3.

Street Trees

Trees that grow between the sidewalk and street or along the road need to be tough to survive. According to Dr. Mark Starrett, street trees must be able to withstand winter salt, compaction, and often limited soil space. Not only that, good street trees must tolerate regular pruning to keep their size manageable and away from overhead power lines. If you plan to plant a tree between the sidewalk and street, he warns, you should check with local authorities before planting. There may be restrictions as to where you can plant and what species are deemed acceptable. Bigger towns like Burlington and Montpelier have city arborists who can give you advice, as do some smaller towns like Woodstock. Burlington also

has a nonprofit organization called Branch Out Burlington that supplies good street trees and helps plant them. Mark Starrett offers these street-appropriate choices:

Callery pear (*Pyrus callery-ana*): Some cultivars of this tree stay narrow, and all varieties put on quite a show in spring, blooming profusely. Its fruit is ½ inch in size but neither edible nor decorative. It's very tolerant of city conditions though not cold hardy in much of Vermont. Starrett recommends 'Corinthian' or 'Green Spire' for their resistance to fire blight, a fungal disease that plagues some Callery pears. Zone 5, or perhaps warmer parts of Zone 4.

Freeman maple (*Acer freemanii*): This is a cross between the red maple and the silver maple that keeps the best traits of each, according to Starrett. It has great fall foliage color and is fast growing but not weak wooded. Zones 3 to 4.

Ginkgo (*Ginkgo biloba*): With its unique fan-shaped leaves that turn a nice yellow in the fall, this shade tree even survives on the streets of New York City. Female trees produce malodorous fruit, so be sure to buy a certified male. Zone 4.

Hedge maple (*Acer campestre*): This handsome, smaller maple is tolerant of salt, drought, and pollution. It branches out low, so it can be used to form a hedge or limbed up and kept in a lollipop shape. Zone 4 or 5.

Little-leaf linden (*Tilia cordata*): One of the best street trees, little-leaf linden has a nice conical shape, medium size, and lovely foliage. Subtle yellow flowers are pleasantly fragrant, and its small winged fruit is almost chartreuse in color, contrasting nicely with the foliage. It's a good shade tree. Hardy to the warmer parts of Zone 3, it should work almost anywhere in Vermont. One of my favorites.

Classic Shrubs

Vermont gardeners have favored a handful of shrubs over the years, so much so that some gardeners consider them trite and tend to avoid them. I disagree. These shrubs are classics: handsome year-round, undaunted by the winters, and willing to grow almost anywhere.

Azaleas and **rhododendrons**: These will grow in full sun or part shade, producing colorful blossoms and shiny green leaves. They like acidic soil and have shallow, fibrous roots; most don't do well if the roots are constantly wet. If you have a heavy clay soil, amend it with peat moss and compost at planting time, and plant the azalea or rhodie in a mound that is a little higher than the surrounding soil for better drainage.

The PJM rhododendrons are bright and colorful and tough as nails. The original PJM is a purple pink, but others now come in a variety of colors, including white. They bloom reliably year after year in Zone 4 or warmer. Retired UVM professor Dr. Norman Pellett likes a white rhododendron, 'Boule de Neige', which translates as "snowball"—and is very winter hardy. Pellett recommends growing all rhodies out of the wind and sheltered from winter sun.

When it comes to cold hardiness, it's hard to beat the Northern Lights azaleas. Some will bloom after winter temperatures of 40 degrees below zero. Few other shrubs will do that. They are, however, gaudy: Some of the Northern Lights azaleas, if their colors were used in clothing, would be suitable for road workers wishing to avoid being hit by traffic.

Forsythia: One of the first shrubs to bloom in the spring, forsythia is known for its dazzling yellow flowers and for the fact that a few plants spaced 5 feet apart will quickly become a dense hedge. I like it best pruned to a vase-shaped shrub, but root suckers will fill in around your original plant if you don't prune them out. Pellett likes the cultivar 'Meadowlark', which is fine leafed, handsome, and one of the most cold hardy. Several cultivars are available that are hardy to Zone 4, though blossoms can be killed by hard winters.

Hydrangeas: With their white snowball flowers in the late summer, these shrubs are popular everywhere, from farmhouse to cemetery. The "peegee" hydrangea is the best known. Its common name derives from the initials of its Latin name: *Hydrangea paniculata grandiflora*. It grows fast, even in poor soil, and blooms when other shrubs are not blooming. Hard to kill. Pick the blossoms in the fall before frost and place in a dry vase for winter arrangements. The *Hydrangea paniculata* 'Tardiva' blooms later and has conical blossom panicles. *Hydrangea paniculata* 'Pink Diamond' is a wonderful variety with smaller blossoms that don't flop on rainy days. Many hydrangeas are hardy to Zone 3, but others only to Zone 4; and the blue ones (*H. macrophylla*) should be considered annuals Ask about hardiness at the nursery where you buy them.

Lilacs (*Syringa* spp.): The common lilac (*S. vulgaris*) is a favorite for its lovely, fragrant flowers and its ability to survive anywhere. It is often seen near the cellar holes of abandoned farmhouses, thriving despite decades of neglect.

Lilacs prefer full sun but will survive anywhere. They flower most profusely in soil that has a neutral pH, so spread

some wood ashes or limestone over their roots. It doesn't really matter when you do this. Three or four coffee cans of wood ashes or limestone distributed around the base of a mature lilac each year is plenty.

Lilacs can live for a hundred years or more but get less vigorous and produce fewer flowers as they age. Prevent this by thinning out the older canes (stems) every few years, cutting them right to the ground. Many of the older varieties send up root suckers— unwanted shoots popping up nearby. Unless you prune suckers out every year, your lilac will spread, becoming a cluttered mess.

There are many species of lilacs and more than 800 named cultivars. By buying several you can extend the season of blooms to six weeks. 'Miss Kim' is a nice Manchurian lilac (*S. patula*) developed at the University of New Hampshire that grows slowly, stays relatively small, and blooms after the common lilacs. Norman Pellett likes *S. chinensis* 'Saugeana' for its lilac-red flowers. Zone 3. Visit the UVM Horticulture Farm or the Shelburne Museum during their lilac days in May, which feature dozens of varieties in bloom.

Roses: Zones 3 to 5 or 6, depending on variety. It's true that long-stemmed English tea roses can be finicky and are best grown as annuals in the colder parts of the state, but there are plenty of good roses are that are fully hardy. The Canadian Explorer series of roses, developed in Ottawa, are hybrid roses that have rugosa roses in their parentage and were bred for hardiness and disease resistance. Rugosa roses, also known as beach roses, are nearly indestructible but have smaller blossoms and short stems. They do have large hips, or seedpods, that can be decorative all winter. I love *Rosa glauca*, a rose with a purplish hue to its leaves. In recent years a trademarked group of roses called 'Knock Out Roses' has

come on the marketplace. These roses bloom all summer, are disease free, and don't seem attractive to insects. Their only flaw? Most have no scent.

Some Lesser-Known Small to Medium-Sized Shrubs

Dr. Mark Starrett of UVM recommends five shrubs that merit more use in the home landscape.

Kalm St. Johnswort (*Hypericum kalmianum*): Small and very round in shape, this shrub displays yellow flowers in July when few other shrubs bloom. Very low maintenance, it rarely needs pruning. Grows in full sun; does well in dry soils. Reaches 2 to 4 feet tall and wide. Hardy to Zone 4.

Large fothergilla (*Fothergilla major*): A slow-growing, medium-sized shrub that blooms early in spring, this one has exceptionally fine fall foliage, with leaves showing great diversity of color from yellow and orange to red and purple—all on one plant. Prefers full sun and well-drained soil. Grows 5 to 7 feet tall and wide. Zone 4.

Red chokeberry (*Aronia arbutifolia*): This native Vermont shrub has white flowers in spring and scarlet foliage and fruit in fall. The fruit, typically avoided by birds, will persist after the foliage drops, extending the season of interest in the fall landscape. The preferred selection of this plant is 'Brillantissima'. It grows 6 to 10 feet tall in sun or part shade and is adaptable to most soils. May spread by suckers. Hardy to Zone 4.

Summersweet or sweet pepperbush (*Clethra alnifolia*): Very fragrant bottlebrush flowers in August make this smaller shrub a great addition to perennial flower beds. Starrett recommends 'Ruby Spice' for its reddish-pink flowers or 'Sixteen Candles', which is white. Sun or partial shade, prefers moist, well-drained soils. Grows 3 to 6 feet tall and wide. Zone 4.

Winterberry (*Ilex verticillata*): This shrub is a Vermont native, growing at the edges of swamps and best known for its bright red berries in the fall and early winter. You must plant both male and female plants to get berries. Starrett likes the cultivars 'Jolly Red', 'Maryland Beauty', 'Winter Red', and 'Sparkleberry', which are readily available at nurseries. He is doing studies to determine which cultivars keep their colors best after repeated frosts. Handles sun or partial shade, wet or dry soil. Grows 6 to 10 feet tall and wide. Zone 3.

Planting for Birds

Birds need food, shelter from Vermont's cold winter winds, and nesting places safe from cats and other predators. Here are a few native species that are important to the birds:

American elder (*Sambucus canadensis*): These shrubby small trees do well in wet places. The fruit is eaten by more than thirty species of birds.

Canadian hemlock (*Tsuga canadensis*): A big tree, it provides nesting and shelter to twenty kinds of birds, some of which eat the seeds.

Highbush blueberry (*Vaccinum corymbosum*): Forget about making pies! Plant a few blueberries for the birds and for the great fall foliage colors.

Staghorn sumac (*Rhus typhina*): Despite the fact that this small tree spreads by root and can take over the landscape, it is an important roadside restaurant for robins and other birds returning in the spring when lunch is hard to find. Plant it where you can contain it by mowing.

White pine (*Pinus strobus*): Pines get to be huge, but the seeds are eaten by more than forty species of birds, and nearly as many use the trees for nesting or shelter.

Final Thoughts

When it comes to planting perennial flowers, I am willing to take a chance that a plant will survive outside its rated hardiness zone. After all, even if it dies I haven't invested much time and money. I'm more conservative when it comes to buying trees and shrubs, however. They cost more, take up more space in the garden, and are a lot more work to plant. Still, I have planted Zone 5 trees and shrubs in my Zone 4 garden, and some have survived. Good soil, good drainage, and a little protection from the winter's north wind help considerably. But a hard winter can kill a tree that you have loved even for a dozen years.

Because Vermont's climate varies considerably, you will have to decide for yourself if you're willing to plant a tree or shrub that is only marginally hardy in your area. If you have a neighbor who has grown the same cultivar, you probably can, too. Just remember: Trees and shrubs take time to reach maturity, so you'd better get planting soon!

Lawns

There is something in most of us that likes a lawn. Perhaps an expanse of green soothes a weary brain or resonates with memories of our childhoods, when we had no responsibilities and could loll about on the lawn picking dandelions, giggling, or rolling down hills.

Lawns are the easiest of all gardens to maintain. We can have a basic lawn without pulling weeds, mulching, or battling bugs. Mowing is the only essential task. Sure, some folks love to keep their lawn weed-free and short, but you don't have to. This chapter will give you some tips to make lawn maintenance easy—so that you can loll about on it if you like.

Chemical companies have done an excellent job of convincing many of us that lawns should look just so: short, uniform, weed-free, deep green. No dandelions, no crabgrass, no clover. Three-step programs to "Weed-n-Feed" are heavily advertised on television each spring, I'm told. Well, think again. You can have a nice-looking lawn with much less work, much less cost, and no possibility of side effects due to toxic chemicals. You can have an organic lawn.

Spring Lawn Care

Most lawns look pretty awful in early April. The snowplows have dumped road sand and gravel along their edges. Leaves and sticks have fallen, wayward dogs have left deposits. As soon as the soil thaws completely and the lawn has dried out, it's time to rake it. If the lawn is soggy, it will compact when you walk on it, so do have patience and stay off until it's dried out.

Getting the lawn clear of debris is important. Grass will absorb sunshine better if it is not covered with dirt or leaves. Fertilizer and compost will start working sooner and more effectively if they are in good contact with the soil.

Despite claims by the fertilizer industry, lawns don't need big infusions of fertilizer to wake up and get started in the spring. Many chemical fertilizers consist of soluble chemicals that will be picked up by your grass almost immediately. If a rainy week follows your weekend application, however, much of the fertilizer will wash away. If you decide to fertilize, buy organic fertilizer and apply the minimum needed. Organic fertilizers have a small amount of soluble fertilizer, but most of the nutrients need to be broken down by soil organisms and are not easily washed away. Warmer temperatures increase biological activity, hence quicker breakdown of organic fertilizers in the heat of summer—just when they are needed. You can spread some bagged organic fertilizer such as Pro-Gro if you are in a hurry to help the lawn green up. But even better, I think, is to add half an inch of compost. This will not only add a variety of micronutrients, it will also introduce beneficial organisms that are lacking in your soil if you've been depending on chemicals. Just drop compost onto the lawn and spread it out with a rake.

Be gentle when you rake the lawn in spring. While the lawn is still dormant it's easy to inadvertently pull up grass. I favor an old-fashioned bamboo lawn rake, but some of the new plastic-tined rakes work well, too. To save labor I rake the mess onto an 8-by-12-foot tarp, which holds several times as much as a wheelbarrow, and drag it away.

If you are intent on having a weed-free lawn—which I am not—you can reduce the number of weed seeds that germinate by spreading corn gluten on the lawn. This is an inexpensive corn by-product sold in fifty-pound bags at garden centers and feed stores.

It is important to apply corn gluten early in the season for the treatment to be effective. Do it in the time between the blooming of forsythia and daffodils in April and lilacs in May. Don't be unrealistic: Corn gluten is not a miracle. Some weed seeds will germinate, depending on your soil conditions.

Brian Steinwand, formerly the liaison with the golf course industry for the Environmental Protection Agency, told me that golf course managers have reported great results after using corn gluten for three years in a row. Weed seeds in the soil don't all germinate at once, so repeated use appears to be necessary.

Lawns that have been treated with chemicals in the past and have relatively little biological activity will not do as well with a

Live Near Water? Don't Pollute!

Excess phosphorus and nitrogen that run off or leach from soil can pollute lakes, streams, and even our groundwater. According to UVM Extension turf expert Sid Bosworth, you can minimize runoff of phosphorus and nitrogen by doing the following:

1. Test the soil of your lawn to see if you need phosphorus or nitrogen before adding any.

2. Use a drop spreader, not a spinner spreader, to apply fertilizer to reduce the risk of spreading it on the driveway or the street.

3. Never fill the spreader on the driveway. Do it on the lawn where spills will not wash into waterways in a rainstorm. Spills can be raked out over the lawn.

4. Never fertilize just before a rainstorm is forecast, as a hard rain can easily wash away most of your fertilizer. Instead, apply fertilizer on a dry day and use a sprinkler or hose to help it settle in.

gluten treatment as an organic lawn. Microbes are needed to break down the corn gluten, releasing peptides that prevent roots from getting established. Unfortunately, corn gluten will also prevent any seeds you intentionally plant from growing, too. If you apply corn gluten in the spring, you should wait to plant lawn seeds until the fall.

Corn gluten has the added advantage of adding some organic nitrogen to the soil. Unlike chemical applications of fertilizer, it won't dissolve and end up in our water systems. It is transformed into usable forms of nitrogen and minerals over time. Corn gluten contains about 10 percent nitrogen by weight.

Spring is also a good time to fill in dead spots or thin places in the lawn. Scuff up the soil surface with a short-tined garden rake and scatter seed over the surface. Flip over a lawn rake so the tines are up, then run it over the seeded area. That will mix the seed into the top quarter inch of soil. Pat it down with a tamper or a board to establish good contact between soil and the seeds, or borrow (or rent) a lawn roller to do larger areas.

It is important to keep newly seeded areas from drying out. You can spread a 1-inch layer of straw over the surface or buy a paper mulch such as Penn Mulch. The latter product comes as little pellets of cellulose that absorb water nicely. Ordinary mulch hay has seeds in it, so it's better to buy straw that doesn't. If the weather is dry, turn on a sprinkler every day until the grass is established.

Getting a Good-Looking Organic Lawn

Paul Sachs of Bradford is the author of three books on lawns and is the owner of North Country Organics, a company that produces organic fertilizers and markets organic products for lawns and gardens. He suggests that if you want a nice lawn without applying chemicals, the best approach is to overseed your lawn once or twice each year. That means spreading a light dose of seed right over the existing lawn.

He recommends doing this after Thanksgiving (or as soon as the ground has frozen) or in early spring before the lawn wakes up. For his display lawn at the factory in Bradford, he also overseeds in September to fill in any spots that have suffered due to heat or drought. Adding seed is "like an infusion of youth in a naturally aging lawn," Sachs says.

According to Sachs, overseeding helps to reduce weed problems because weeds can't get established if there is a thick canopy of grass that shades them out.

Another key to success is to let the lawn grow a bit taller than you might prefer, say to 3 inches. Conventional wisdom is wrong, Sachs explains: You don't have to cut more often if you leave the grass longer. The rate of growth is the same. And a newly mown lawn looks good no matter what. Avoid scalping the lawn at all costs, he advises: Take just a third off, even if you've been away and the lawn is overly long.

According to Dr. Sid Bosworth, UVM Extension agronomist and turf expert, cutting the lawn at 2½ to 3 inches reduces stress on the lawn and helps to minimize most lawn problems. Taller grass has more leaf area, which means more photosynthesis can take place, producing deeper root systems. Taller grass also shades out weeds and crabgrass. And it feels better underfoot. But as Paul Sachs points out, roots can only go down so far if the soil is compacted—no matter what else you do to improve the lawn.

How can you tell if your lawn is compacted? Try this simple test. Get a screwdriver with a 6-inch shaft and try to insert it into the soil. You should be able to push it in, using moderate force, up to the hilt. If you can't, your lawn is compacted and needs help. One solution is to rent a core-aerator machine. This engine-powered machine will punch little holes in the lawn, removing small plugs of grass that will loosen up compacted soils and allow compost or fertilizer to get down to the roots of the grass. In small areas you can aerate with a fine-tined pitchfork. Some people wear golf spikes to aerate the soil, but that sounds silly to me, and Sachs says it won't accomplish anything. Applying compost after aerating will jump-start the recovery process.

The Best Seed Varieties

Kentucky bluegrass is thought by many lawn professionals to be the gold standard of turf grasses for golf courses and parks. Although Kentucky bluegrass requires the most sunshine, fertilizer, and watering, it is rhizomatous, meaning it spreads by rhizomes, or roots, so it will fill in bare spots and hold up well to foot traffic. If you want an easy-care lawn, Paul Sachs recommends no more than about a quarter of a seed mix should be bluegrass.

Perennial ryegrass is quick to germinate in the spring. It is a clumping grass, so it won't spread to fill in bare spots. It is also not as winter hardy or drought resistant as bluegrass.

Fine fescues are the lowest maintenance turf grasses. They are clumping grasses that require little to no fertilizer or watering. Some dwarf fescues require less frequent mowing, too. There are several varieties of fescues, including red, chewing, hard, tall, and dwarf varieties.

What is the best blend of grasses for an easy-care lawn in full sun? Sachs suggests one

Shake It, Shake It Baby

If you are buying a lawn seed mix that contains clover seeds, you need to invert the bag or box and shake before using it, says Paul Sachs. Clover seeds are tiny and dense and sift down to the bottom of the bag. When you get to applying seed from the bottom of an unshaken bag, you are in danger of getting mostly clover in one portion of your lawn. Believe me, I've done it.

with about 35 percent tall fescue, 15 percent chewing fescue, 15 percent hard fescue, 15 percent perennial ryegrass, 10 percent Kentucky bluegrass, and 10 percent red fescue. A blend gives you something that will do well under most weather conditions on any given year. Furthermore, any monoculture—such as a pure stand of bluegrass—is more susceptible to attacks by insects and diseases.

I like to see some Dutch white clover in the mix because clover will add nitrogen naturally—so long as you apply no herbicides to the lawn, which will kill clover. Nitrogen-fixing bacteria can live in the roots of clover, taking nitrogen from the air and converting it to a form that is available to plants in the soil. Translation: You won't have to fertilize the lawn as frequently—or at all—if you add white clover to the mix.

For folks who really want the classic look of a high-maintenance lawn and are willing to fertilize three times a year, a mix of 50 percent Kentucky bluegrass, about 25 percent perennial ryegrass, and 25 percent fine-leaf fescue should do the trick.

Shady Lawns

As the trees around your house get bigger and spread more shade on the lawn, your lawn will start to lose its vigor. In addition to the shade they create, trees spread roots farther into the lawn, stealing moisture and nutrients from the lawn. Maple trees are notorious for spreading their roots long distances, particularly Norway maples. If the shaded soil stays moist and is acidic, mosses will show up uninvited and stay. But be open to the idea that moss isn't all bad. You don't have to mow it, and it stays green. Don't rake it, though, as it pulls up easily.

Realistically, you'll probably need to plant more than one mixture of grass seed on your property. For areas of shade, buy a mix that has about 70 percent fine fescue, 20 percent perennial ryegrass, and perhaps 10 percent Kentucky bluegrass of a shade-tolerant variety.

Weeds

Weeds are, by definition, tough plants growing where you wish they wouldn't. In lawns weeds and crabgrass grow where turf grasses struggle—especially where the soil is compacted. They take over when they can outcompete the lawn grasses. Here are some suggestions to minimize weed problems:

1. Get a soil test done, then follow the recommendations. Soil pH is important and easy to fix. The ratio of calcium to magnesium is important, too. A ratio of 7:1 to 10:1 is good. There are two kinds of limestone. Add *dolomitic* limestone if your soil is low in magnesium, but use *calcitic* limestone if there is already plenty of magnesium in your soil. If the pH is right but calcium is low, add gypsum, which won't affect pH.

2. Add compost each spring and fall to attract earthworms and other beneficial organisms. Half an inch will help.

3. Keep the mower blade at 3 inches. Tall turf grass will shade out some weeds, particularly in the spring.

4. Stop walking where the lawn is compacted and struggling. You could put down pavers or stepping-stones so that people will walk on them instead of the grass. Use a sharp knife to cut out the lawn in the shape of your stepping-stones, and set them into the lawn at the level of the soil surface. That way you can run right over them with the lawn mower.

5. Plant creeping thyme or another ground cover where the lawn won't grow. Thyme smells lovely when you step on it, and some varieties stay very low.

Summer Lawn Care

It's summertime and you will have to mow. You may need to water (though I don't), and you will need to decide how to use your grass clippings.

Mowing and Mowers

Mow the lawn when it needs it, not on a fixed schedule such as every Saturday morning. Keep the blade sharp so that it cuts, not tears, the blades of grass.

Keep the blade up high, preferably 3 inches. Grass survives by virtue of making its own food by photosynthesis. The more leaf area, the more food a grass plant makes. The more food, the better roots it will grow. Longer, deeper roots survive droughts and stresses better and create a spongier lawn.

What type of mower works best? It depends. Sheep were the original lawn mowers, and I've tried them. I used a portable electric fence, moving it around the property every few days. But that gets old—fast. Sheep are more trouble than they are worth, despite the free fertilizer. They don't cut the grass evenly and were always trying to eat my flowers.

Planting Sod in Vermont

Buying sod or having it installed is expensive. Sod is grown in farms that provide perfect growing conditions for sod to grow: just the right amount of sun, water, and fertilizer. Sod comes in densely planted rectangles that can be laid down like floor tile. The problem is that you probably won't be able to give it the same care that the sod companies do. Like a drug addict going into recovery, your sod may have some tough times at your house. I don't recommend sod, but April and May is the time to install it if you decide to use it.

Old-fashioned push mowers were invented around 1830 and were the way to mow lawns for about a hundred years. The labor of pushing them encouraged people to keep lawns small. Now unless you have just a tenth-acre lot and like exercise, you probably should have a power mower of some sort.

If you have an acre of lawn or more, a riding mower is worthwhile. It doesn't make sense to spend more than two hours a week walking behind a lawn mower. A riding machine can cut mowing time in half simply by being twice as wide.

Generally the riders are faster than push mowers, too. A basic 10-horsepower mower will do for three acres or less, if you just want to mow. If you're interested in adding other accessories, you'll need at least a 15-horsepower mower.

The turning radius is important if you have lots of trees, rocks, and flower beds to mow around. A mower with a 16-inch turning radius can mow tight to a 32-inch diameter island, but a 20-inch radius machine will require you to back up and take a couple of tries to mow around that bed.

Watering

I never water my lawn, and it doesn't die. Like any lawn it goes dormant during long periods of hot, dry weather and loses some of its green color. That's normal. It revives after the drought. Lawns cut close to the ground will scorch and turn brown before lawns with longer grass.

It is possible to keep your lawn a gorgeous green right through August. Golf courses do it. They also water every day.

When to Water

Lawn experts agree that watering in the morning is better than in the evening. That allows the day's sun and wind to dry the leaves before nightfall, minimizing fungal problems that wet leaves can develop in hot, humid summer nights. Watering in the heat of the day just wastes water due to evaporation.

A lawn needs more water as temperatures rise. A minimum of an inch of rain per week is needed to keep a lawn looking green in a dry period, or more than that if you wait until the lawn is parched. Sandy soils need more than clay soils. If you use a sprinkler, put out an empty tuna can about 8 feet from the sprinkler and time how long it takes to deliver an inch of rain. Check the distribution of the sprinkler with cans elsewhere, too. After a watering, the soil should be moist down to 6 inches.

Grass Clippings versus Thatch

Lawn jockeys, the guys who ride around on huge lawn mowers for a living, are forever lamenting the presence of thatch (a layer of dead grass) on lawns. They want to catch every blade of grass and power rake your lawn to get rid of thatch. Don't let them.

Grass clippings that fall on a biologically active lawn, one that has not been treated with chemicals, will be broken down by the organisms in it. The clippings are rich in nitrogen, and they return that nitrogen to the soil. Grass clippings and clover in a lawn can produce enough nitrogen to keep a low-maintenance lawn looking good without fertilizers. Chemically treated lawns have a much harder time processing clippings and may accumulate thatch. Thatch can also be a sign your lawn service has added too much fertilizer: Your lawn is growing so fast that it can't decompose fast enough. If thatch gets to be more than a half inch thick, it needs to be raked out. Half an inch or less can act as mulch, holding in water and keeping weeds from germinating.

Pests and Diseases

A good healthy lawn shouldn't be plagued with diseases. In the spring many lawns will have what appear to be dead spots, but these generally recover without treatment. Sometimes a spring lawn will have patches of snow mold or other fungal diseases. For advice, contact the Master Gardener Helpline (see chapter 14).

Lawns that are given too much chemical nitrogen fertilizer grow fast and have weak leaves. The excess nitrogen makes grass attractive to pests and diseases. I once interviewed Joe Mooney, the groundskeeper at Fenway Park in Boston for thirty-five years, who kept the grass under an inch long and pumped it up weekly with fertilizers. But I visited the underground storehouse of fungicides and insecticides that he needed to keep the lawn healthy, and that approach is not for me.

Moles get blamed for a lot they would never think of doing, such as eating the roots of your lawn. If you have moles, it is probably a sign that you have lots of grubs—their meal of choice. You can repel them by using a commercial mole repellent, or you can make your own (see the "Henry's Magical Mole Mix" sidebar). But if you have lots of grubs, they will be back.

Japanese beetle grubs or cutworms may live in your lawn, eating grass roots and creating dead spots if too many are present. If you think your lawn roots are being eaten by them, cut out a 1

Henry's Magical Mole Mix

A friend of mine had a dog that dug up her small lawn because he wanted to catch the moles there. I made up a simple mixture of castor oil and soap and spread it using a watering can, and the moles packed their bags and never returned. And the dog was out of the doghouse.

Mix one tablespoon of castor oil (available at local pharmacies) with two tablespoons of liquid soap (not dish detergent) in a blender until it gets stiff like shaving cream. Then mix in six tablespoons of water. Add two ounces of this mixture to two gallons of water in a watering can. Sprinkle the diluted mixture on the lawn.

When you buy your castor oil, make sure it is the old-fashioned type, not the new, improved, unscented type.

foot square of sod, peel it back, and count the grubs. If you have more than ten, you have a problem.

One organic approach to killing lawn grubs is to buy beneficial nematodes, a variety known as Hb nematodes (*Heterorhabditis bacteriophora* is the species). According to Paul Sachs, Hb nematodes will attack some 250 species of grubs but will not affect earthworms, though the nematodes may infect some beneficial insects that have the same life cycle as the targeted pest. Hb nematodes come on a moist sponge that you immerse in water; then you spray or sprinkle the liquid on the lawn. The best time to apply nematodes is in April, before grub larvae turn into beetles, or, better yet, in August and September when the eggs are hatching. The application of Hb nematodes, like any biological control product, is not a guaranteed success.

Japanese beetles and their grubs will be back to your property each year if you have roses or other things that attract them (grapes, crab apples, etc.). The long-term solution may be to buy a bacterium known as milky spore (*Bacillus popilliae*) and apply it to the lawn. There is some debate over the effectiveness of milky spore this far north, however, and no definitive studies have proved its efficacy. Some entomologists do not believe it is effective; I have heard plenty of anecdotes indicating that it is effective. I do know it's expensive to buy.

Milky spore is not a quick fix: It takes three years for this biological control to become fully effective, and in urban areas it works best if an entire neighborhood agrees to do treatments. If not, Japanese beetles will fly over the fence to your roses from the neighbor's yard.

Fall Lawn Care

September is a better time to plant grass seed than the spring, whether seeding a new lawn or filling in dead spots. Autumn soil temperatures are warmer than in the spring, and that means grasses will germinate more quickly. Fall in Vermont is often rainy, which also helps new lawns get established.

Limestone is slow to move through the soil, so adding it in the fall gives it time to work its magic through winter. If you can scratch limestone into the lawn with a rake and get it below the surface a little, it will be closer to the crown, or growing point, for both roots and leaves. For new lawns, lightly rototill limestone and compost into the top 4 inches of soil before seeding.

Mow less often in the fall as the lawn slows down. But the last two mowings should be a little shorter. In late October reduce blade height by ½ inch, then do that again for the final mowing. Long grass can get matted down by winter snows and thus be more likely to get snow mold or other fungal diseases.

Final Thoughts

Lawns are as American as apple pie. But try to rethink your attitude about them a little. Does it really matter if you have a few dandelions? And what is wrong with clover? Wouldn't you rather be puttering in the vegetable garden or dozing in the hammock on a hot day than raking out thatch?

Sometimes having patience and putting up with a problem may be a better solution than buying a chemical or biological control—unless the Queen is coming and you absolutely must have a perfect lawn. Me? If it's green and I can mow it, it's a lawn.

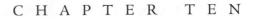

Invasive Plants

Invasive plants are foreign, nonnative species that have become pests. In some cases they came to America by invitation. Others arrived unnoticed, stowed away with cargo on ships or planes. A few may even have traveled as seeds in the cuffs of travelers' trousers. Some were smuggled in by overzealous plant collectors. In any case, they found the New World to their liking and flourished. Most invasive species have no natural predators here, so there are few natural mechanisms to keep their numbers in check.

Vermont is blessed with a cold climate that keeps some, like the notorious kudzu vine, from settling in. Others, like Japanese knotweed, are perfectly happy in the Green Mountain state. The sale of some invasives have been banned by the state, while others that are just as aggressive have not.

This chapter will identify the bad boys and encourage you to get rid of those that have found a home on your property. You may be fond of some plants on the Vermont list of prohibited species (formally called the Noxious Weed Rule). Other invasive plants may be pesky but seem near impossible to get rid of. Don't worry: Even if you harbor some fugitives, the Vermont Agency of Agriculture won't be sending the plant police to your door. They *will* prevent garden centers from selling those on the list, however.

158

What Makes a Plant an Invasive?

Invasive plants reproduce rapidly and take over wild habitats, out-competing native plants by stealing light, water, and nutrients from less-aggressive plants such as our beautiful native wildflowers. Most invasives produce large numbers of seeds that are distributed by birds, by wind, or by water. Often the seeds and fruit of invasives are less nutritious for wildlife than natives. In most cases, invasives are nearly impossible to remove or eradicate once established, and most have extensive root systems that preclude simply pulling them up.

The Official List of Prohibited Invasive Plants in Vermont

The Vermont Agency of Agriculture, Food and Markets adopted a plant quarantine rule to regulate the importation, movement, sale, possession, cultivation, and/or distribution of certain invasive plants, some of which are listed below. These species are found growing in Vermont and pose a serious threat to the state. Aquatic plants such as Eurasian milfoil are also on the list, but because they are not relevant to home gardeners, they aren't included here You can find an expanded list of noxious plants by typing in "Invasive plant species Vermont" into your search engine on the web.

Common name	Scientific name
Trees and shrubs	
Amur maple	*Acer ginnala*
Norway maple	*Acer platanoides*
Tree of heaven	*Ailanthus altissima*
Barberry	*Berberis* spp.
Burning bush	*Euonymus alatus*
Honeysuckles	*Lonicera x bella*
	Lonicera maackii
	Lonicera morrowii
	Lonicera tatarica

Glossy buckthorn	*Rhamnus frangula*
Common buckthorn	*Rhamnus cathartica*

Vines

Japanese honeysuckle	*Lonicera japonica*
Black swallow-wort	*Vincetoxicum nigrum*
Oriental bittersweet	*Celastrus orbiculatus*

Garden plants and weeds

Goutweed	*Aegopodium podagraria*
Garlic mustard	*Alliaria petiolate*
Wild chervil	*Anthriscus sylvestris*
Flowering rush	*Butomus umbellatus*
Japanese knotweed	*Fallopia japonica* or *Polygonum cuspidatum*
Purple loosestrife	*Lythrum salicari*
Common reed	*Phragmites australis*

What Do Invasives Do?

Bill Guenther, a Windham County forester, has seen firsthand what Japanese barberry can do: In 1996 he visited a site with a few barberry bushes alongside a stream but not in the nearby woods. When he visited the same site seven years later, the barberry had invaded the pine woods, creating a thorny barberry thicket so dense that even wearing heavy jeans and chainsaw chaps he could not walk through it. The affected area covered several acres and was expanding.

Kathy Decker, a forest protection specialist with the Vermont Department of Forests, Parks and Recreation puts it this way: "Do you like maple syrup and fall foliage? If so, get rid of the Norway maple, because it has the potential to take over the habitat of the sugar maple." Unfortunately, she notes, most people can't differentiate between the two, and once established the invasive Norway maples are hard to remove.

What Can *You* Do?

For starters you can learn to identify the invasive species and try to eliminate them on your own land. Next, avoid planting any of the species on the prohibited list. Don't accept gifts from neighbors of plants that are invasive. If you see a large infestation of an invasive or a plant on the watch list, you may contact Elizabeth Spinney at the Department of Forests, Parks and Recreation at (802) 477-2134 or e-mail her at elizabeth.spinney@vermont.gov to let her know about the plants or to ask for her advice.

If you are a city dweller, you may assume that because there are no forests nearby, it shouldn't matter if you grow invasive species. Not so. Wind and birds can distribute seeds, and rainwater runoff can carry seeds through subsurface drainage systems to an outlet in a natural environment. Seed from your tree can end up in streams, rivers, and ponds. Thus even city dwellers can help control the propagation of invasive plants by getting rid of theirs.

Control of Invasive Species

Each species of invasive has its own characteristics and recommended control methods. These methods can be grouped into the following categories: mechanical control, biological control, and chemical control.

For the average home owner, the first method, mechanical control, works just fine. However, forester Kathy Decker recommends an IPM (integrated pest management) approach—including chemical herbicides in small doses where other methods fail on stubborn species. The IPM approach takes into consideration the nature of the pest, the extent of the infestation, and multiple control tactics.

Whether to use chemicals or not is a choice you will have to make. I recommend trying hard with mechanical controls: If you persist, I believe you can beat most pest plants.

Mechanical Controls

Mechanical controls involve pulling up, cutting down, mowing, or blocking the sunlight from the invasive plants. Sometimes a combination of those techniques works well.

Have a patch of Japanese knotweed? Even herbicides won't kill an established patch. You can't dig out all the roots—I once talked to a guy who used a backhoe and went down 8 feet, trying to get out all the roots but couldn't. But digging out most of the roots is a good first step. It will deplete much of the stored carbohydrates the plant needs to send up new shoots.

Next? Think lawn mower. Once you have the stalks (and some of the roots) removed, plant grass seed. Mow it every week and the invasive's roots will not get recharged. Its stems will continue to grow for years, but if you mow it, you will eventually win. If you don't want lawn there, think weed whacker. Go out there every week and think of someone you don't like as the knotweed king. Cut him (or her) down, with a grin.

For trees and shrubs, cutting down the culprits is relatively easy. Unfortunately some will send up new shoots from their roots time and time again. If you keep after these sprouts, eventually they will use up their stored food reserves, but this can take years. At the very least, cutting down most woody plants annually will prevent them from setting seed—the first-year growth should not produce flowers and seeds.

Instead of cutting down trees like buckthorn that respond by sending up dozens of root sprouts, I've used an easier way to kill it: With a pruning saw I've cut rings around the trunk in two places 12 inches apart, double girdling the tree. According to one authority, it important to cut through the cambium but not cut all the way to heartwood, as cutting heartwood may stimulate root suckers to sprout. By girdling the tree, you slowly starve the roots. This method takes three years to succeed, but it does work. If you have a multistemmed tree like a buckthorn, it takes some persistence to get to every trunk.

Pulling small trees is best. Little ones—in their first year or two—will uproot easily. With age (yours and the sapling's) it gets harder. There is a tool for pulling saplings called a Weed Wrench. I've used them, and they really work. A Weed Wrench of the proper size allows a 150-pound office worker to pull out trees that otherwise would be impossible to yank. It has a gripping mouth-like part and a long handle to provide leverage. It will pull young buckthorn, getting most of the root system. It does disturb the soil, however, so dormant buckthorn seeds there may germinate. Getting rid of an invasive species on your land is an ongoing, not one time, effort.

Unfortunately the Weed Wrench company recently went out of business. There are alternatives being produced, though I have not tried any. One is called The Uprooter (www.theuprooter.com); another is the Pullerbear (www.pullerbear.com).

> ## Is It an Invasive Norway?
>
> To see if maple trees growing wild near you are Norway maples, do this simple test: Snap off a leaf at its attachment point and look at the stem. If it oozes a milky sap, it's a Norway maple. The leaves also tend to be broader and larger than sugar or red maple leaves. There is a purple-leafed cultivar called 'Crimson King' that is very popular as a street tree. Seedlings from it generally have green leaves and are not as obvious as the parent trees.

Biological Controls

Biological controls for some invasives are vastly superior to other methods, including those "quick-n-easy" chemical controls. Controlling purple loosestrife is one of those cases. Purple loosestrife grows in wet areas, forming thick colonies that roust other plants and the wildlife that depends on a diverse ecosystem. The beautiful blossoms in August are wonderful. But it's an invader and was once hard to eliminate. A European beetle has been introduced to control it.

Dr. Richard Casagrande of the University of Rhode Island has been working on biocontrol of invasive species for many years. He told me that when gardeners hear that new species of insects have been introduced to help control invasive plants such as purple loosestrife, there is a knee-jerk reaction: "Great. And when they've finished eating the loosestrife, what's going to happen next? Will they eat my delphiniums—or my peonies?"

The process of introducing foreign insects to combat these pests is tightly monitored. The University of Rhode Island has quarantine labs that are almost as tightly controlled as the perimeter around the White House. Here's what they do:

First, scientists look at how the invasive species performs in its native land. Purple loosestrife came from Europe in the early 1800s—probably in soil used as ballast in ships—but it is not a problem there. Why not? It evolved there, and over time some 120 species of insects learned to love it. Of these, fourteen are host specific, meaning that they eat it—but nothing else. A few of these insects were brought to quarantine labs to test the following: Will they eat related species of the target plants or plants that share a habitat? Will they attack any of our major crops such as corn, wheat, and soy?

If you've ever tried to dig out purple loosestrife, you know that it has an amazing root system that will challenge even the strongest back. Scraps of roots left in the ground will start new plants. Not only that, each mature plant produces millions of tiny seeds every year, so even if you did poison or pull one, the soil is full of tiny time-release capsules—seeds—that will start the process all over again next year, and the year after that, and so forth. Even burning plants will not solve the problem. But it can be kept under control with the use of introduced beetles.

Since 1994 beetles that eat purple loosestrife have been successfully reducing stands of this exotic. They reduce the numbers of plants to around 10 percent of pre-introduction levels; as the numbers of plants drop, so do the number of the predator beetles.

Similar efforts are under way to control phragmites, that tall reed grass that has such beautiful plumes in wetlands and along roadside ditches. There are two varieties of phragmites. One is a native, noninvasive type that is not common; the other is the same genus, but a foreign species. Scientists are seeking insect controls that would attack the invasive and leave the native variety—and are making good progress to this end.

Cary Giguere, the Vermont Agency of Agriculture pesticide program manager, told me about an interesting biological control that has been developed for deciduous woody plants that re-sprout after being cut down. It is a naturally occurring fungus, *Chondrostereum purpureum*, that is spread on the stumps of pest trees right after they are cut down. It has been used in test plots in Vermont since 2004, and according to Giguere it has "pretty good efficacy." The fungus is produced in Canada and is sold under the trade name Myco-Tech. It has been used along right-of-ways and in evergreen woodlots. This biological control is still in the early stages of testing, but it may turn out to be a boon to landowners fighting infestations of things like buckthorn or honeysuckle. According to the Environmental Protection Agency website, no reports of adverse effects have been reported on birds, wild mammals, fish, insects or other invertebrates, or aquatic plants. It is approved for use in Vermont but is not yet available.

So what can the home gardener learn from all this? First, realize that help is on the way in the form of biocontrols. Second, recognize that herbicides for plants (and insecticides for insects) are not fully effective—there is no miracle cure for your problems. Yes, you can kill loosestrife with a spray, but loosestrife generally grows near streams or marshes where herbicides are prohibited.

Can you buy beetles to eat up the purple loosestrife near your stream? Probably not. As organic gardeners, we have to accept that we are not in total control of the environment, and that sometimes we have to wait or endure some losses. Biological controls do work; they have made some exotic pests such as birch leaf miners into nothing more than minor annoyances. There are already places where purple loosestrife is no longer a problem. And scientists are working hard at finding safe, reliable ways to control pest species without chemicals.

Chemical Controls

There are a few new herbicides that have been approved by OMRI (the board that approves products for use by organic farmers). Matran-2 contains clove oil, and Xpress contains thyme and clove oils and acetic acid. They are most effective on young broad-leaved weeds and probably of little long-term value in killing invasives. They essentially burn the leaves, stopping photosynthesis for a period of time. They do not kill the root systems, and like any strong chemical—whether made from plant extracts or synthesized in a chemical plant—they must be used with great care. They can harm other living beings. They are most effective if sprayed when the air temperature is over 70 degrees.

Of the chemical herbicides, those containing glyphosate are thought to be the best, meaning that they kill plants well but are less harmful to other living beings. Roundup, made by Monsanto, is one brand name. These herbicides are sprayed on leaves or painted on cut stems of woody plants. The chemicals travel to the root system, where certain metabolic processes are then shut down, killing the entire plant.

Chemical herbicides are not without risk, despite industry claims. In a review of the technical literature done by the *Journal of Pesticide Reform* (volume 24, number 4), more than forty studies were cited that showed glyphosate herbicides caused harm. Some of them cited genetic damage in laboratory tests with human cells as well as in tests with lab animals. Others showed a link with non-Hodgkins lymphoma, miscarriages, and attention deficit disorder. Still other studies showed damage to the immune system of fish and abnormal development in frogs.

Not only are there risks from the active ingredients in herbicides, the herbicides also contain "inert ingredients" that may pose risks. The inert ingredients help a pesticide to stick to the leaves of plants or to spray more easily. The composition of inert ingredients in a product is considered a trade secret and need not be listed on the label. Some ready-to-use herbicides are up to 98 percent inert ingredients. The review cited above listed a dirty dozen—twelve commonly used inert ingredients—that have been shown to cause harmful side effects.

If you decide to use an herbicide, be sure to wear a long-sleeved shirt, long pants, and a hat. Buy a good mask or respirator to protect yourself from inhaling the product. And apply it on a day with no wind.

Alternative Plants

If you remove invasive plants, you will probably want interesting substitutes for them. Chapter 8 lists excellent trees and shrubs for Vermont, and chapter 7 features wonderful perennials. Best of all, go to your local family-owned garden center and talk with someone knowledgeable who can recommend plants that will do well in your neighborhood. Public gardens and nurseries with display gardens, listed in chapter 13, are good sources of ideas for replacements—though some of these gardens and nurseries may still harbor a few of the pest plants in their display gardens.

Norway maple, barberry, and burning bush are the most common invasives that were deliberately planted in the landscape. Here are some substitutes for them:

Norway maple:

Red maple (*Acer rubrum*): Zone 3; 40 to 60 feet, fast growing. Will do well even in soggy, poor soil. Red buds in the spring and red foliage in fall are nice. Ask at the nursery if the plant you buy has been grafted onto a rootstock, and avoid those that have—they sometimes fail at the graft union.

Ginkgo (*Ginkgo biloba*): Zone 4; 50 to 80 feet, medium to fast growth. Great urban tree, as it is salt and pollution tolerant. Interesting fan-shaped leaves.

Pin oak (*Quercus palustris*): Zone 4; 60 to 70 feet, fast growing. Survives well in heavy clay soils and wet conditions. Nice pyramidal shape.

Red oak (*Quercus rubra*): Zone 3; 60 to 75 feet, fast growing. Prefers well-drained soils. Nuts great for wildlife.

Barberry and burning bush:

Common ninebark (*Physocarpus opulifolius*): Zone 2; 6 to 10 feet, spread 6 to 10 feet, medium to fast growing. 'Diablo' has nice reddish purple foliage, as does 'Summer Wine', which stays smaller, about 6 feet; 'Dart's Gold' has yellow green foliage; all can be striking and have nice white or pinkish flowers in midsummer.

Large fothergilla (*Fothergilla major*): Zone 4; 6 to 10 feet tall and wide, medium rate of growth in youth, slow at maturity. White bottlebrush flowers in spring last three weeks. Exceptionally nice fall foliage colors; often each leaf is a slightly different color.

Japanese red maple (*Acer palmatum*): Zone 4; size varies from 6 to 25 feet, slow growing. In southern climates this is a full-sized tree. I have one more than thirty years old that is only 8 feet tall and wide. Rich, dark, wine-colored leaves.

Highbush blueberry (*Vaccinum corymbosum*): Zone 3; up to 12 feet tall and 8 feet wide, slow growing. Don't worry about birds eating your berries—let them. Grow it as a decorative shrub. Nice spring flowers, blue fruit, good fall color.

Final Thoughts

Inertia is the root of many problems. For years I've been aware that the bird-planted bush honeysuckles on my property were invasives. But there was always too much to do, too many "more important" tasks on the list of chores I tackle each weekend. So the bushes lived on. Finally, in 2006, I started digging them out.

One side benefit I discovered after pulling half a dozen of these large shrubs was this: All of a sudden I had room for more plants. I had pretty much run out of gardening space, and removing the thugs gave me more places to plant.

Remember, too, that invasive plants can more than double their populations every year. Some, like purple loosestrife, can disperse a million seeds annually. Even if only a few of those seeds grow, each of the offspring can yield another million seeds each growing season. It's important to stop the geometric progression.

Lastly, avoid so-called "sterile cultivars" of invasive plants. Some varieties of purple loosestrife, barberry, and others are said to be sterile hybrids and safe to plant. Don't bet on it. Hybrids can revert to their parent plants and turn on you, so stay away from them all. Better safe than sorry.

Garden
Solutions

CHAPTER ELEVEN

Tools of the Trade

When the first farmers began to plant seeds thousands of years ago, they probably had only one or two tools. Perhaps a pointed stick for planting, or a sharpened stone or shell for slicing woody stems. But now gardeners are faced with an amazing array of tools to choose from. Some are great; others may languish in the barns and sheds of gardeners who find the tools don't really work as well as they had wished. Let's look at the tools you need.

The Basics

You will need a shovel, a hoe, a garden fork, a weeding tool, a lawn rake and a short-tined garden rake, a pair of pruning shears, and a wheelbarrow. In addition, you will need a bucket, a watering can, and, depending on the size of your garden, a hose and a watering wand. I like to buy good quality tools, tools that my grandchildren will use long after I'm gone. Big Box stores often sell flimsy tools with thin metal and weak handles. That may make them less expensive and lighter to use, but they won't hold up for prolonged use. I find that family-owned hardware stores and garden centers generally have a good selection of tools—and a range of prices. You get what you pay for.

Shovels and Spades

I use the terms spade and shovel interchangeably. They come in several types: short-handled, long-handled, pointed, or with a square end. I suggest that you select something that is sturdy, but not too heavy. Pointed shovels are generally easier to use for digging than square-ended spades. Most short-handled shovels have a "D" grip that you can grab onto. Long-handled shovels do give you more leverage, but are heavier. Some gardeners swear that long-handled shovels are easier on their backs, but I say it's all about how you use them.

Shovels and other tools are now sold with either wood or fiberglass handles. I like the feel of wood, and have several tools with wooden handles that I use often, even though they are over 50 years old. Fiberglass is generally promoted as tougher, less susceptible to breakage than wood—but you should never break a handle of either kind if using it properly. I once was given a shovel with a steel handle, used it to pry out a big rock, and ruined the handle!

I have had fiberglass handles develop long cracks in them after just a dozen years of use. Hickory is the best, toughest wood for handles, and ash is good, too. Cheap spades may use less expensive foreign woods of poor quality.

I apply a coat of boiled linseed oil once a year to wood handles to keep them from drying out. I also try real hard not to leave tools out in the sun or rain, or in the back of my pickup truck when not in use.

Specialty Spades

The drain spade, also called a transplant shovel, has a long, narrow blade—mine is about 16 inches long and 5 or 6 inches wide. It is a great tool for transplanting. I loosen the roots of a flower or shrub by pushing the spade under the plant at a 45 degree angle and prying gently. I use the spade to pry the roots all around the plant until the root ball is loose and can be removed easily.

I also have a half-sized spade. This I use when I am working on my knees to plant bulbs or flowers. It is lightweight, and is great for shaping a hole I have started with my full-sized spade, or cleaning out a little more soil to deepen the hole. It's so light that I can use it with one hand. Its handle is just 18 inches long.

Hoes

Conventional hoes are useful for moving soil in the garden. I use one to smooth out the walkway in my vegetable garden, or to drag soil from the walkways into my mounded, raised beds. It can also be used to cut off young weeds if you keep it sharp.

Weeding hoes come in dozens of varieties. The best is the scuffle hoe or stirrup hoe. The business end of this hoe is shaped like the letter "D" and has sharp edges on both sides of the blade. That way you can cut off weeds pushing or pulling. With a little practice, you can get a lot done fast with this, slicing off weeds just below the soil surface.

Farmer and writer Eliot Coleman of Maine has collaborated with Johnny's Selected Seeds (www.johnnyseeds.com) to develop and market a line of tools that work very well. They sell several weeding hoes, all of them good, including the stirrup hoe, the trapezoid hoe, and the collinear hoe.

To save your back when hoeing, stand straight up and hold the hoe with your thumbs up. Pull toward yourself, slicing off the tops of the weeds. Never hoe by leaning forward with thumbs down—it's a prescription for a sore back (even though it is the grip most people start with). And if you must lean forward, keep one foot well in front of the other.

Garden Forks

Everyone needs a garden fork. These tools have four tines 10 to 12 inches long. The fork is easily plunged into the soil by putting your weight on it, just like a shovel. Pull back on the handle, and you loosen the soil and any weed roots, making them easier to extract.

A garden fork is sort of a poor man's rototiller—it does the job of loosening the soil. It doesn't break the soil lumps into fine powder the way a machine might, but that's good. Worms and soil organisms have made their homes at the depth they like best, and don't want to be buried deeply or brought to the surface by a revolving blade. I don't recommend rototillers. A fork can be used to break up big clumps, and I use my favorite weeding tool to stir up the soil a bit when I actually plant a perennial or a tomato.

Weeding Tools

Weeds are the gardener's nemesis. They persist, year after year. Unlike most garden plants, weeds can grow in almost any soil and send roots deep, far and wide. If you hear roots snapping when you pull a clump of witch grass, you probably know that the grass may grow back again from the scraps of roots you didn't get. A good weeding tool is able to loosen the soil around a weed so that when you pull it, you get all the roots. It should also be comfortable in your hand, and light enough that your hand is not tired after an hour of weeding. Precision is important, too.

My favorite weeder is the CobraHead (www.cobrahead.com). It has a single steel tine that is shaped like a long curved finger on a blue recycled plastic handle. The tip of the tine is flattened and

made sharp to easily slice through the soil and grab onto weeds. I use it to get under weeds, tease out long roots, stir up the soil to plant … just about anything that I'd do with my fingers, I do with this tool. It's 13 inches long, weighs 9 ounces. It's also left hand neutral.

The Cape Cod Weeder is another single-tined weeder for precision weeding. It has a straight handle with a small blade on a right angle. This comes in right- and left-handed versions. I used one for years—until I got a CobraHead.

Planting/weeding knives come in a variety of names (one is the hori hori knife), and most feature a tough broad blade with one serrated edge, handy for cutting back perennials at the end of the season. The blade is useful for digging out tap-rooted weeds. Sheaths are recommended.

Hand trowels can be used for a variety of functions from digging out weeds to planting flowers. Everyone should have one.

The dandelion weeder is another classic for digging out tap-rooted weeds. It has a forked blade on the end of a long, round shaft. It's lightweight, easy to use.

The three-pronged cultivator is another old-fashioned tool that comes in a variety sizes and shapes. It can grab onto weeds, allowing you to pull them out.

The pavement or crack weeder is a must-have if you have a brick or stone walkway set in sand. It is a thin metal L-shaped weeder that will get in cracks where nothing else can.

I recommend buying tools at your local garden center. That way you can handle them, see how they feel. But if you don't have a store nearby, check out Johnny's Selected Seeds (www.johnny seeds.com), Lee Valley Tools (www.leevalley.com), and OESCO (www.oescoinc.com). All three sell good quality tools.

Rakes

Two types of rakes are needed: a short-tined garden rake (sometimes called a rock rake), and a long-tined lawn rake. I use a garden rake to move soil, smooth out beds, rake out weeds and stones from the soil, and level off beds.

There are three basic types of lawn rakes: those with plastic, metal, or bamboo tines. I like all three. Bamboo rakes are light and great for raking dry fall leaves. Unfortunately, over time some of the tines will snap off. Plastic rakes are also light, but a little stronger. They come super wide (30 inches) to small (8 inches). The toughest rakes have metal tines, and I find myself reaching for a metal rake most often. I use one to rake up wet leaves, heavy grass clippings, and soil. I also have a metal rake that can be adjusted from narrow to wide. I find it very good for working in flower beds.

Pruning Shears or Saws

When working in the garden I wear a leather holster to carry a pair of pruning shears. I use them to tidy up flowers, trees, and shrubs. Wearing them on my hip, I don't have to go the house or barn to find a pair, they are always with me.

There are two kinds of pruners: bypass and anvil. The blades of bypass pruners work like heavy-duty scissors. Kept sharp, they will make clean cuts on branches up to half an inch in diameter. The anvil pruners have a sharp blade that closes down on a flat area of soft metal or hard plastic that is stationary. The blade essentially crushes and severs the branch, but never makes as clean a cut as one made by a bypass pruner. They're often much cheaper than the bypass pruners, but no professional pruner would ever use them.

Loppers are handy for pruning larger branches. I have a pair of 32-inch geared loppers made by Fiskars (www.fiskars.com) that I love. The gears allow me to cut hardwood branches up to an inch and a half, a great time-saver when compared to using a pruning saw.

Pruning saws come in many sizes and styles. A simple folding saw is fine for most jobs. Saws today have tri-cut blades that are very efficient, but cannot be sharpened. I don't recommend bow saws for pruning because they can't get into tight spaces.

Last thoughts: Don't ever use pruners or loppers on branches too large for them. You will "spring" the blades (bending them away from each other) and they will never work as well again. And this: Buy good quality. Cheap pruners are not worth a penny.

Wheelbarrows

One of my first memories in life is riding in my grandfather's wooden wheelbarrow as we raced to the barn ahead of a thunderstorm. I have a similar wooden wheelbarrow made by an Amish man in Pennsylvania (Spring Valley Woodworking), but I use it more for decoration than for work.

The classic wheelbarrow with one wheel in front and a large metal or plastic bin is a useful tool for carrying weeds, soil, compost—almost anything. The bins come in a variety of sizes; I like the 6-cubic-foot size, but gardeners with smaller gardens might prefer a 4-cubic-foot wheelbarrow. I favor wheelbarrows with the metal bins because they are sturdy, though good plastic versions are nice, too. They are considerably lighter and don't rust. The advantage of the classic wheelbarrow is that you can push it almost anywhere because the single wheel allows you to turn on a dime.

I recommend buying a tube for the tire of your wheelbarrow, because otherwise you will eventually get lots of flats. My neighborhood mechanic supplied and installed the tube in mine.

Bigger wheelbarrows of the classic style also come with two tires in front. I find them harder to turn and don't recommend them.

For big loads I have a Muller's Smart Cart (http://shop.mullers carts.com) that is great for heavy and bulky loads. The axle is centered under the load so that it feels light to the touch and turns easily. It has a tubular aluminum frame and a big plastic bin (7 cubic feet). You can easily remove the bin from the frame so that you can wash the dog in it, or transport messy stuff to the dump in the back of your car. I like the model with wide wheels, which is rated for 600 pounds; the wire wheel version is rated for 400 pounds. Everything about this cart is well designed. It's more expensive than a standard wheelbarrow, but worth it. I keep mine outdoors all summer without problems.

Wooden garden carts (plywood, actually) generally come in two sizes, large (13.6 cubic feet, carrying capacity 400 pounds) and medium (6.5 cubic feet, carrying capacity 300 pounds). These are nice carts, but you end up lifting more of the load when the cart is full than you would with the Smart Cart. They're great for carrying leaves and hay, but not dirt, firewood, or rocks. You should keep this plywood cart indoors when not in use. For carts made in Vermont, visit www.cartsvermont.com.

There are all kinds of plastic bins on wheels available inexpensively (under $100) at the Big Box stores, but I don't think they would hold up well for prolonged use. I also have a folding metal garden cart for storing in small garages (the Tipke 2100 folding cart; http://bonjourlife.com/fold-it-garden-cart/).

Watering Cans

Everyone needs a watering can. Hoses are great, but newly planted seeds in the ground can be dislodged by a heavy stream of water from a hose. Little seedlings, too, can be disturbed by a hose. I don't use liquid fertilizers much, but when I do, I need a watering can.

Watering cans come in all sizes, colors, and designs. For ease of use, always get one with a handle that goes from front to back, not side to side. The former type is easily used with one hand, the other is not. Plastic is fine. Make sure you can take off the "rose" or part that distributes the water in a fine spray. You need to do this to clean out dirt and leaves. Also look for a top opening that is large enough to insert a hose with wide nozzle on it, or to pour in liquid fertilizer.

Buckets

Hardware stores sell standard 5-gallon pails for under $5. Get one. You need them for soaking plants before planting, carrying a few weeds to the compost pile, carrying hand tools, etc. You may need more than one.

I have "tub trugs," too. Everyone is selling these bright-colored food-grade recycled polyethylene containers in various colors and sizes, up to 10 gallons. They are flexible and tough, have built-in plastic handles, and are great for carrying or mixing things. I even fill one with water, squeeze the handles together to form a spout, and use it to water transplants if no watering can is handy.

Hoses

Cheap hoses tangle and break. Good hoses don't. Buy the best you can afford. Rubber hoses are heavy and expensive, but seem to last forever and kink less. If you need a long hose to get to your garden, don't buy a 100-foot hose, buy two 50-footers. There will be times when you want something shorter, and there is no point in lugging all that heavy hose.

Drain your hose in the fall, and store in the garage or barn.

Watering Devices

Don't buy a pointy brass nozzle to fit on the end of you hose. Or do, if you want to wash your car. But plants need gentle streams of water that can best be delivered by a watering wand. These devices have long metal handles with a rose (water sprayer) on the end. The best wands are made by Dramm, but many knock-offs are sold, too. Go for the best. Why? They have figured out how to aerate the water so that lots of water can come out, fast, but gently. My wand allows me to walk along and get water where I want it: on the ground, near the plants, not on the foliage.

I don't recommend overhead watering devices, as they wet the leaves, which can encourage mildew or mold, particularly if used in the evening. If you are going away and need to water, you could use an overhead sprinkler or get soaker hoses and arrange them around plants that need watering. Soaker hoses ooze water instead of delivering a spray. They can get clogged, and are not a perfect solution to watering. In my experience they don't survive years of use.

If you attach your hose to a watering timer, it will deliver water on a programmable schedule. If you do so, be sure to test out the system well for a week before going away.

Other Paraphernalia

Comfort while gardening is important. Get kneepads, a lightweight hat, and garden gloves. I spray my garden hat with insect repellent during bug season, and it keeps away a lot of insects. Kneeling pads are fine if you can't find kneepads that are comfy.

Final Thoughts

I know that buying a complete set of tools to start up can be an expensive proposition. Perhaps you can start by going to yard sales—there are always a few tools available. You can skimp along with a weeding tool, a garden fork or shovel, and a garden rake the first year. Ask your family for any tools that they don't need. I treasure tools my grandfather used. I see the patina on the wooden handles and I know it was made with his sweat. And when you buy tools, get good ones so that, hopefully, years from now, your grandchildren will inherit not only your love of gardening, but some fine-quality tools they can use.

CHAPTER TWELVE

Coping with Pests and Diseases

Each of us, organic gardener or not, has the inherent urge to kill anything that threatens our garden. Bugs? Slugs? Ugly fungus? For decades we Americans have been using the nuclear option: spraying plants with toxic chemicals to rid ourselves of whatever offended us. Now, as gardeners get better educated about the side effects of many sprays, folks are looking for less-toxic alternatives.

This chapter will not only share with you some alternatives, it will explain *why* your plants will do better on a pure organic regime. And if the furry, four-footed critters are taking more than their fair share of your garden, there are ideas in this chapter to deal with them, too.

The Disease Triangle

Three factors are involved in causing infectious plant diseases, explains Ann Hazelrigg, plant pathologist at UVM. There must be a pathogen, or disease-causing fungus, bacterium, or virus. Next, there must be a susceptible plant. Stressed, weakened plants are much more susceptible than healthy ones. Lastly, environmental factors that favor development of the disease must exist. Many fungal diseases, for example, require a wet leaf surface to infect a plant. If you can eliminate even one of the three factors, the disease will not develop.

Most plant diseases in Vermont are caused by fungi, organisms that do not have chlorophyll and so can't make their own food by photosynthesis. Fungi are organisms that develop a diffuse, branched body; they reproduce by spores and depend on plants and animals for their food. Mildews and molds are common fungal diseases. Contrary to popular belief, however, most fungi are not disease causing, and some have symbiotic relationships with green plants (that is, relationships that benefit both parties). For example, tree roots benefit from mycorrhizal fungi that share soil minerals with trees and get excess sugars from tree roots in return.

Bacteria and viruses can also cause diseases, but these are much less common.

Some scientists believe that plants that have been given too much soluble nitrogen fertilizer (to make them grow fast) are more disease prone than organically grown plants. Fast growth is softer, weaker, and more susceptible to attack by fungi or bacteria. Just as a run-down, sleep-deprived, malnourished child will get every cold or flu passing through school, plants growing in poor soil or pumped up on chemicals will fall prey to diseases more easily.

Disease resistance has been bred into many modern hybrids. Many tomatoes, for example, are bred to resist verticillium, fusarium wilt, or root-knot nematodes. Some are resistant to all three. Read your seed packets carefully or ask about the plants you are buying. If you've had problems with plant diseases in the past, get resistant varieties. Resistance does not mean your plants cannot get the disease or be attacked by the parasite. It is just less likely.

Environmental factors can often be manipulated to minimize problems. Certain fungal diseases can only successfully penetrate leaves if the leaf surfaces are moist, for example, so watering in the morning is better than in the evening for preventing those kinds of diseases. Dividing big clumps of flowers so that air circulates better can help, too. Staking tomatoes to increase air circulation is another way to minimize the leaf spot diseases that attack this plant every summer.

Give a plant what it needs for optimum growth and the chances for success are better. Sun-loving plants should be grown in the sun. Growing them in the shade may make them more susceptible to disease.

Integrated Pest Management

University of Vermont Extension takes an integrated pest management (IPM) approach to controlling and preventing plant diseases and minimizing losses to insect pests. The goal of IPM is to reduce the use of chemicals and the costs of using them. An IPM approach does not always eliminate the use of chemicals, but it seeks to promote the judicious use of chemicals (the least possible and the least toxic). Some chemicals such as rotenone are derived from plants—and hence approved for organic gardeners—but rotenone would almost never be recommended in an IPM program because it is highly toxic and has a long residual effect.

The basic tenet of IPM is simple: Learn as much as you can about pests and diseases that affect your plants. If you can identify them, know their life cycles, and attack them at their weak spots, you will do just fine, most years. The IPM strategy is to use the least toxic approach to any problem and to promote good growing techniques so that diseases don't take hold.

But the bottom line is this: If you're a lousy grower and you're not careful, it doesn't matter if you are a traditional grower, an IPM grower, or an organic grower—you'll still be a lousy grower. So do your homework and be a good grower.

Preventing Plant Diseases

Once a disease has infected your plants, it's generally too late to do anything about it for this growing season. Plants don't recover the way humans do. Once a plant is showing symptoms of disease, it's usually too late to cure it, though you can take steps to minimize spread of disease. We can't cure the leaves that are already spotted. Either we live with the imperfection or we remove the infected parts or the whole plant.

Generally home gardeners should avoid using chemicals, says Ann Hazelrigg of UVM: "Home gardeners are not dependent on the garden for their livelihoods the way farmers are. I like to promote organic practices."

The best approach is to prevent disease from occurring. This is done by growing vigorous, healthy plants that will naturally resist diseases, says Hazelrigg. Her recommendations include:

1. Clean up the garden at the end of the season. Most pathogens overwinter on plant tissue, so you need to remove dead plants. She recommends putting diseased plants in the trash or burning them. Burying is another possibility, as soil organisms will break down most pathogens.

2. Keep in mind the disease triangle. If you can eliminate even one of the three factors needed for a disease to take hold, it will not infect your plants.

3. Grow disease-resistant varieties of plants that have been problematic for you in the past. There are many good cultivars of flowers and vegetables that are less prone to disease, though this does not make them disease-proof.

4. Accept the fact that there is no "silver bullet." Each year will have different growing conditions, and some years disease will be worse than others.

Hazelrigg's lab will diagnose plant diseases for a fee of $15, but she suggests that you first contact the Master Gardener Helpline at (800) 639-2230. Helpline volunteers can diagnose many diseases, and if they can't they will pass on a sample to her lab for diagnosis—but for free!

Remember that soil rich in organic matter will, in general, promote healthy plants. Farmers and gardeners who add compost to their soil every year swear that this helps to prevent diseases. At present it is not known if the soil microorganisms in compost produce substances that inhibit disease, if they outcompete disease-causing organisms, or if they just help plants to grow well and fight off diseases themselves.

Common Diseases and What You Can Do for Them

Powdery mildew: This is the white powder that appears on the leaves of your phlox, bee balm, lilacs, and other plants. If it has been a problem in the past, you might try some prevention:

- This fall, clean up any debris beneath the plants. Spores (fungal seed equivalents) overwinter in plant debris. Burn, bury, or put infected plants in the trash. Any spores left on the soil will probably be eaten up by soil microorganisms.

- Divide large clumps of mildew-prone perennials in the spring. Or prune to allow better air circulation. Move plants to full sun if possible.

- Avoid watering in the evening. Water on leaves is not required for powdery mildew to develop, but high humidity is a factor.

- Select mildew-resistant cultivars. A good garden center can help you select replacements for plants that become infected every year.

- If you see an outbreak starting, make a solution of one tablespoon of baking soda and a drop of liquid soap to a gallon of water, and spray. That should help to keep powdery mildew from spreading. Commercial organic sprays of potassium bicarbonate such as Milstop and Remedy can also be used safely. You will need to reapply on a regular basis, probably once a week.

Fungal diseases on tomatoes: Tomatoes often lose their lower leaves to fungal diseases such as early blight and septoria leaf spot; lower leaves turn brown and curl up, eventually spreading to the entire plant. Rotating the location of your plants each year can help, but crop rotation is not the solution that it is often touted to be, as spores can spread by wind or water. What can you do?

- Mulch with grass clippings or leaves. This will minimize splash up from the soil.

- Purchase resistant or tolerant varieties.

- Stake or cage your plants to keep them off the ground and to allow good air circulation.

- Keep detailed garden records to help you select healthy varieties in future years.

- If all else fails, and the problem greatly reduces your crop, move your garden. Select a site as far away as possible, and dig up the sod to start a new tomato patch.

Apple diseases are another common frustration for gardeners, but up to 90 percent of disease can be eliminated with good orchard sanitation. Apple scab is a common fungal disease that mars the skin of apples but rarely makes apples inedible. Apple scab spores overwinter on leaves under the tree, so rake up leaves in the fall. Black rot and canker spores overwinter in fruit, so rake up downed fruit, too; use a bamboo pole to knock off any apples that have not fallen. Rake again in the spring, then put down a layer of mulch.

Apple scab spores germinate in wet weather about the same time that flower petals fall. The warmer the temperature, the more quickly the spores can infect a tree. Fruit or buds can only be infected while wet, so pruning to open up the tree to breezes and sunshine will dry surfaces more quickly, helping to minimize infections.

Biological Aids for Disease Control

Three brands of commercially available products can be used for disease control. They may help under certain conditions, but they are not a foolproof method of preventing disease.

Serenade is a product that contains a commonly occurring soil bacterium that has antifungal characteristics. The bacterium, *Bacillus subtilis*, penetrates and destroys the disease spores but does not harm beneficial insects or wildlife. Use it against powdery mildew, gray mold, early blight, bacterial leaf blight, botrytis neck rot, walnut blight, downy mildew, fire blight, scab, bacterial spot, and pin rot. It is said to stimulate a plant's own disease-fighting mechanisms as well. It is approved for use by organic gardeners and has no restrictions about when to use it or on what.

Messenger contains naturally occurring bacterial proteins that are good for increasing plant vigor and resistance to diseases. The active ingredient, harpin, was discovered by scientists at Cornell University, who extracted it from the bacterium that causes fire blight in fruit trees. It apparently stimulates plants to mount their own defenses against disease. The manufacturer recommends using it before diseases occur.

Plant Shield contains *Trichoderma harzianum*, a soilborne microorganism that works as a biofungicide. It is used to prevent several types of root rot and also to prevent foliar fungal diseases if sprayed before the onset of diseases. It will not stop an infection once it has started.

Identifying and Diagnosing Plant Diseases

Some problems, like powdery mildew, are easy to identify. But most of the time you'll need some help.

My favorite book is *Insect, Disease & Weed I.D. Guide: Find-It-Fast Organic Solutions for Your Garden*, edited by Jill Jesiolowski Cebenko and Deborah L. Martin. It has good illustrations and organic suggestions for dealing with problems.

A great resource for gardeners is the UVM Extension Master Gardener Helpline. Even though a phone diagnosis is tough to do, the volunteers in the UVM Master Gardener program staff this toll-free helpline, and usually someone can give you a good idea of what your problem is. The Master Gardeners can be reached at (800) 639–2230 or (802) 656–5421. The helpline is generally open in summer Monday to Friday from 9:00 a.m. to noon. In winter the hours are Monday, Wednesday, and Friday 9:00 a.m. to noon. Because this service is provided by volunteers, hours are subject to change each week. Sometimes volunteers are busy and you have to wait, so leave a message and callback number if need be.

Environmental Problems

Not all plant problems are caused by diseases. Some are caused by environmental factors: things like weather as well as things we gardeners may have done wrong, such as letting rock salt get on plants in winter. A severe drought can affect the health of trees and shrubs for three to five years. Plants rely on stored energy, and if they fail to thrive because of drought (or overly wet conditions), they do not produce all the energy they need for good growth and resistance to disease. Drought predisposes trees and shrubs to cankers and tip blights and puts them in a generally weakened state. This is another good reason why you should water newly planted woody plants and perennials regularly their first year, and additionally in subsequent years if rains are not adequate.

Plants can also be burned by careless use of chemical fertilizers. Sprinkling a strong fertilizer around a plant and failing to mix it in to the soil can dry out tissue and even kill the plant. Too much chemical fertilizer in a planting hole can burn the roots. Plants should be watered before fertilizing to avoid burning roots.

Slugs, Bugs, and Things That Go Munch in the Night

Slugs? Japanese beetles? Tent caterpillars? Potato bugs? These are creatures that gardeners love to hate. These critters turn normal gardeners into vengeful killers. Asked for gardening New Year's resolutions, one reader of my weekly gardening column wrote, "I resolve to beat my record of killing 368 slugs in one day! Yes, I counted each and every one that fell under the spell of my garden pruners!"

Some gardeners lose their resolve and spray toxic chemicals when their roses are threatened or the striped cucumber beetles eat the first leaves of their little cukes. Don't. There is much you can do to keep insects off your plants, to repel them, or to trap them; then there are the time-honored methods: pick and drown them, or simply squish them.

I am rarely bothered by insect pests, and I have always been an organic gardener. Coincidence? Perhaps. But I attended a lecture by a research scientist at Ohio State University, Dr. Larry Phelan, who offered an explanation for what I have observed. Phelan wanted to see if organically grown plants attracted insect pests differently than those grown using conventional techniques. He collected soil from two farms that were across the road from each other. The soils were identical except for how they had been tended for the past several years. One farm was organic, the other conventional.

To reduce other variables, Phelan brought the soil to his greenhouse and potted it up in large containers. He then grew corn in containers, adding chemical fertilizers in some, fresh cow manure in some, and composted manure in others, using both types of soil for each method. When the corn was at the appropriate size, he released corn borers into the greenhouse and watched what happened.

The corn borers preferred the corn grown conventionally. Additionally, the long-term history of the soil mattered. The soil from the organic farm had higher levels of organic material in it and consistently was less attractive to the borers—even if used with chemical fertilizers.

Why should this occur? Plants evolved over millennia getting their nutrients through the soil food web, depending on the symbiotic relationships between plants and soil microorganisms, explains Phelan. Chemical fertilizers are imprecise, providing nitrogen for fast growth, but often giving too much nitrogen or providing it all at once. When a plant gets too much nitrogen, he says, the excess is stored in the form of amino acids, the building blocks of protein. This is like candy for kids or drugs for addicts. Insects can detect it and go to the source. In contrast, soils rich in organic matter provide nitrogen and other needed nutrients in a slow, steady stream—the way Mother Nature does it.

In another experiment Phelan grew soybeans hydroponically (in water), varying the amount of nutrients present. The soybean looper preferred plants that were nutritionally out of balance. But not just nitrogen mattered. Iron, boron, and zinc levels were important, too. And of course, those elements are not present in conventional fertilizers, which offer only nitrogen, phosphorus, and potassium containing compounds. Good soil enriched with compost should have everything your plants need.

All in all, the best way to prevent insect attacks on your crops is by using good cultural methods. First and foremost, learn how to be a good gardener. Healthy plants are less attractive to pests than stressed plants. Stressed plants often emit pheromones (chemical signals) that attract insects.

What can you do? Rotate crops in the vegetable garden, use physical barriers like row covers to keep bugs off your plants, and clean up and get rid of debris from plants that have been the host to insect pests. Vermont state entomologist Alan Graham says that it's important to figure out what the problem is, and what your threshold is—how much damage can you tolerate. He recommends an integrated pest management approach (IPM) that uses the least toxic means possible. Graham says handpicking potato beetles, for example, is tedious, but can help a lot. And he says, don't panic.

Good Bugs

One reason not to use broad-spectrum insecticides, whether of botanical or chemical origin, is that they kill the good insects along with the bad. Just because a spray is approved for organic farmers doesn't mean that you should automatically reach for it. Rotenone, pyrethrum, and other sprays are touted as "safe for organic gardeners," but they will kill parasitic wasps, ladybugs, and other good insects. And many of the good insects are not at all obvious to most of us. They are often small and unobtrusive. I say, "Just don't spray!" Graham says, "Just because it's organic doesn't mean you can double the dose."

To attract good bugs, grow lots of flowers and even allow a few weeds. Chickweed, for example, is an early blooming weed that provides pollen and nectar for ladybugs before the aphids and other pests are available for their lunch. I grow flowers in and around my vegetable garden, and these plants attract and feed some of the insects that keep my garden relatively pest free.

Bad Bugs

Tarnished plant bug: This insect is little known by Vermont gardeners, but is one of Vermont's worst insect pests. It often causes poor fruit production that is blamed on weather, particularly for peppers and eggplants. These insects have been known to attack some 500 different species of vegetables, fruits, and flowers. Its sucking action on stems makes small fruits fall off and may lead to deformed fruit and masses of seeds in strawberries.

Tarnished plant bugs are about a quarter of an inch long, light brown, and variously spotted. The white, yellow, and black spots give the insect a tarnished appearance, but there is a clear yellow triangle, marked with a black dot on the lower third of each side.

Think you have them? Put down a piece of white paper under a plant and shake it. The bugs move fast, so you have to be quick— or make the paper sticky enough to catch them. Tanglefoot is a commercial product you can apply to paper to trap them.

There is not much an organic gardener can do to kill or repel these bugs, but you can protect plants with row covers, which will keep the insects off. Row covers are made of lightweight synthetic fabric that allows air, sun, and moisture to pass through, but not bugs. Wire hoops are needed when covering plants like peppers; for cucumbers I just lay the fabric on the ground and pin it down over the seedlings. Insect-pollinated plants like peppers and cukes need to have row covers removed when they blossom, but eggplants do not need insects for pollination and can be protected all summer. Reemay and Agribon are commonly sold brands of row cover. (Read more about using row covers in chapter 2.)

Japanese beetles: Don't buy those sex-scented trap bags or you'll have the entire neighborhood's beetles eating your plants. Handpick the beetles early in the morning, shaking them into a container of soapy water. I have had good luck repelling (or confusing) them by spraying with a solution of liquid fermented salmon fertilizer. Garlic Barrier, another commercial product, helps, too. In either case it's harder to repel them once they have found your roses, so try to do it before bloom time. But you can't necessarily just mask the odor of a plant to fool the insects.

Potato bugs, aka Colorado potato beetles: Handpicking really works, you just need to go do it every day for a couple of weeks when the bugs first appear. Most important, look for orange egg masses on the underside of leaves. If you have a big problem every year, consider using Bt. It's a natural bacterium (*Bacillus thuringiensis*) that can be diluted with water and sprayed on plants. Bt is not a contact poison, it is a biological control that sickens the larvae. You can also cover plants with row cover until mid-season. The beetles feed not just on potatoes but also on eggplants and others in the same family. But Bt must be sprayed when the larvae are very young and reapplied every year to be effective.

Because potato beetles overwinter as adults in protected areas, one way to foil them is to rake up all your potato vines into the middle of the garden, providing a nice winter home for them. Then have a midwinter bonfire and kill them all! Or you can skip growing them some years to reduce their numbers the next.

Tent caterpillars: These guys are like teenagers: They like to sleep all day, so they eat at night. Remove the tent and its caterpillars during the day and drop the whole mess in a bucket of soapy water. I swab it off with a rag or knock it down with a stick. The problem, of course, is that you can't reach the tents high up in trees. But even if your tree is completely defoliated, it probably won't die. I've seen trees refoliate from dormant buds after being stripped of leaves.

There is only one generation of tent caterpillars each year. The caterpillars can be controlled with a product that is approved for use by organic gardeners, Dipel. It contains a specific bacterium strain (*Bt kurstaki*) that will control most caterpillars. It is not toxic to us, fish, birds, or other insects, though I recommend wearing a mask when spraying anything. The hitch is that the caterpillars have to eat the Dipel. So you must spray it on leaves they will eat. It works better for younger caterpillars. It can be bought at most garden centers. Properly stored, the same container of Dipel can be used for several years.

Striped cucumber beetles: These pests are about ¼ inch long and love to defoliate the first leaves of cucumbers, pumpkins, and squashes. I've also found them in the flowers of mature plants. Their "saliva" spreads diseases that can shorten the life of your plants, too. Now when I plant the seeds, I cover the hill with row covers. Or you can plant extra seeds so that even if the beetles get some of your squash or pumpkins, other plants will survive and thrive.

Tomato hornworms: These are big green caterpillars up to 4 inches long. The moths resemble hummingbirds in their habits. Certain parasitic wasps naturally attack these critters, so if you see what look like grains of rice on a hornworm, leave the worm alone. Those are cocoons of the parasitic wasps. You might move infested hornworms away from your tomatoes to allow the larvae to mature elsewhere. Otherwise, pick and drop the hornworm into soapy water.

Lily leaf beetles: The beetles are so pretty that you might want to use them as earrings: bright red with black trim, about ¼ inch long. Their larvae, in contrast, are disgusting—they carry their excrement on their backs to deter birds (and organic gardeners).

Dr. Richard Casagrande and his coworkers at the University of Rhode Island have introduced parasitoids from Europe—tiny wasps—that reduce the lily leaf beetle populations. The parasitoids are doing the job near test sites in Rhode Island and Massachusetts. In the meantime, I have given up on growing Oriental and Asiatic lilies. I found I couldn't keep up with the beetles, even if I picked every day and I am unwilling to spray poisons. Organic gardeners sometimes have to admit defeat.

Plum curculio: You may not recognize the name, but this insect's larvae have the potential to practically eliminate your fruit crop, and in some parts of the state it does. The larvae attack developing fruit (apples, plums, pears, peaches, cherries), causing up to 90 percent of the fruit to drop off the tree in late June and early July. The fruit that does stay on the tree is disfigured.

The best treatment is to spray trees with a water solution of kaolin clay after petal drop. This product (sold as Surround) coats the fruit with a dusty barrier, and that changes the way the adult insects perceive the fruit so they don't lay eggs on it, or not as often. Particle film barriers like Surround can work on broccoli to keep off cabbage worms, too. It means more thorough washing is needed at harvest time, and your crops look dusty. Unfortunately, Surround can be harmful to your lungs if you inhale it. It is available from Gardens Alive (see chapter 14).

Spotted winged drosophila: In 2011 or 2012 this new pest arrived in Vermont. It is an Asian fruit fly that attacks ripe and ripening fruit of brambles (raspberry and blackberry), strawberry, blueberry, grape, cherry, plum, and peach, and many species of wild berries. Other fruit flies eat over-ripe or rotting fruit, so are not a problem. These fruit flies arrive late in the summer, so early season berries and fruit are better choices. The flies are tiny, just $\frac{1}{12}$ of an inch, and are not easy to detect, though traps are now available. Fine netting may be one way of keeping them off a few plants, but no easy solution has been found for big plantings.

Deer ticks: This is the worst pest because it can affect you directly, not your plants. These tiny ticks carry Lyme disease and a number of other diseases that can knock you for a loop. I know, I've gotten Lyme and one other infection and ended up in the hospital after one bad bout. UVM Extension has pictures of these ticks and recommendations, just search online for "UVM deer ticks."

I've read that May, June, and October are the worst months, but they are out there all summer, too. If you get a bite, try to remove the entire tick with tweezers, or see your doctor if the head breaks off and stays under your skin. If you develop a bull's-eye or rash on your skin, see your doctor. Antibiotics early on can save you from much discomfort. You can prevent bites by tucking your pants into your socks, and then spraying your legs and shoes with DEET-containing repellent. Check yourself daily after working in the garden! Disease can penetrate your skin, so don't handle the ticks, use tweezers.

Slugs: These pests are not insects but mollusks. There is a slug bait that is safe to use around pets and rated for use by organic gardeners. It's called Sluggo, and it works. However, I recently read a report that alleged that Sluggo may not be as benign as it claims to be, and that the "inert" ingredients may be toxic. Beer in saucers will catch and drown them, but they don't deserve the beer. Handpicking works. Or spread a band of wood ashes or sharp sand around young seedlings—slugs hate to crawl over it—though that treatment is only partly effective. Slugs feed mostly at night during dry weather, and you may be able to trap them during the day if you put down boards for them to crawl under.

Other Insect Pests to Worry About

State entomologist Alan Graham filled me with apprehension as he listed other pests that are headed toward Vermont—or have recently arrived. These include the hemlock wooly adelgid, a pest that attacks hemlocks. Watch for small dots of white fluffy "cotton" on the needles during the winter. Adelgids in southern New England have devastated hemlock populations, so the border is closed to imports.

Then there is the emerald ash borer that gets under the bark of ash trees and fatally girdles the trees by eating the cambium layer. Watch for leaf dieback on top branches and D-shaped insect exit holes on the bark. These borers are a real problem in the Midwest.

Lastly, the Asian longhorn beetle prefers maples for breakfast, lunch, and dinner. Yikes. One day we may all have to use synthetic syrup. Look online for photos of these beetles.

Graham asks anyone who sees one of these three pests to please go to www.vtinvasives.org/tree-pests/report-it. You can see the pests there, and report an infestation. A few wooly adelgids have come to Vermont but they have been controlled. The other insects haven't been spotted—yet, but Graham says it's "only a matter of time." Fortunately cold winters knock the pests back some.

Furry Pests

Deer, rodents, raccoons, and rabbits: They all want to help in the garden by getting rid of your extra vegetables and flowers. You don't have to shoot them, trap them, or fence them out, though those solutions do work. My mild-mannered corgi, Daphne, helps to scare them away from my garden. Here are a few other possible solutions.

Deer are pests throughout the state, but often more so in towns and villages. Hunters can't shoot deer downtown, and the deer seem to know it. There is also less natural forage, so they're hungrier.

In areas of moderate deer pressure, I've had good luck repelling deer with coyote urine, which is available at garden centers. I just hung special plastic bottles (that have holes for the odors to escape) every 8 feet or so around a garden; inside each are cotton balls soaked with coyote urine. Deer are creatures of habit, so if they get the idea that coyotes are around, they'll go elsewhere, and not come back—until next year.

Another solution for deer is the electric fence and peanut butter trick. I know people who put out a single band of electric horse

fence on fiberglass poles, about 30 inches off the ground. They spread peanut butter on pieces of aluminum foil, and then use clothes pins to attach them to the "hot" strand. Deer lick the peanut butter and are shocked. It's an easy solution and you can turn it off or take it down while in the garden.

If the deer population density is high enough, they can't be deterred with anything less than an 8-foot fence. Fences really work. Of course, they are laborious to install and expensive. Just how much do you value your tomatoes?

Woodchucks and squirrels: I've had good luck trapping these rodents in Havahart traps (www.havahart.com) and releasing them in the woods far from anyone's home. It's important to get the right size trap—you can't catch a squirrel in a woodchuck trap, or vice versa. For woodchucks you need one 36 inches long with a 12-by-12-inch opening; squirrels need one with a 6-inch square opening about 16 inches long. The traps are expensive; some town animal control officers will lend you one.

It's best to place a trap for woodchucks in one of their pathways near their den, if possible. Bait it with fresh fruit (apples, watermelon) or vegetables (beans are great) that they can't get in your garden at that time of year. You probably won't catch them with beans if you have a row of beans for them nearby.

Squirrels I catch with sunflower seeds, though I hear peanuts work, too. Cover the cage with a towel after you catch an animal so it won't freak out until you release it. I always leave them with a snack when I release them, and I won't trap them at the end of summer or in the fall after they have stored their food for the winter. Even so, I realize that trapped animals have a low chance of flourishing somewhere else and only catch them when there is a severe problem—like the year red squirrels started running into the house to steal dog food. I relocated about thirty squirrels that year and have never had a problem since. One or two? Fine. I can live with that.

Check with your local animal control officer or police department before releasing trapped animals. It may be illegal in more-populated towns.

Raccoons: I've heard these are wily devils, but I've never had a problem with them, probably because I've always had dogs. You can catch them in a Havahart trap or scare them off with a radio with an all-night talk-show format. I'm told you actually need two radios on different stations to keep them away. An electric strand places 12 inches above ground will work, too.

Rabbits: I've heard that fencing is the only way to be sure to protect your lettuce from Mr. MacGregor's nemesis, Peter. Use mesh with a 1-by-2-inch grid, and bury it 6 inches in the soil; it needs to go up 18 to 24 inches.

Voles and mice: Fruit trees can be killed by hungry rodents that chew bark off all the way around, girdling them in winter. Surround the trunk with ¼-inch mesh called hardware cloth. Mouse traps baited with fruit-flavored chewing gum will catch them, too.

Final Thoughts

Gardeners are constantly interfering with Mother Nature's plans. If we weren't here, she wouldn't be growing lilies, lilacs, or lettuce on our plots. Not only that, we humans have introduced pests and diseases from other continents that have no natural enemies. Both these factors affect our success. We need to accept some losses and realize that we cannot—even with the help of chemicals—control or eliminate every problem.

I firmly believe that I have fewer pest and disease problems than my friends who have not yet become organic gardeners. I try to grow healthy plants, but then I let Mother Nature have a hand in how things turn out. So far, so good. And I'm willing to give up growing a few things to avoid those chemicals that might poison our environment even a little bit.

CHAPTER THIRTEEN

Vermont Gardens to Learn From

Visiting gardens is a wonderful way to learn about plants and designing a landscape. All of us, and not just beginners, can learn from others, particularly from public gardens that have the staff and resources to grow plants that we might never have heard about or seen. Because there are few public gardens in Vermont, I have included in this chapter some of the garden centers that have nice display gardens, too.

Burlington Area

University of Vermont Horticultural Research Center. Known to its friends as the "Hort Farm," this is an incredible collection of mature trees and shrubs as well as perennials and fruits. More than 700 kinds of ornamental trees and shrubs are on display, including some—such as their small liquidambar (sweetgum) trees—that are being tested for zone hardiness for the first time anywhere in Vermont. It is a true research station, so little regard has been paid to layout and design, but there is much to learn here. There are specimens of trees seen nowhere else in Vermont.

The Hort Farm is just under a hundred acres and features several special collections, including 120 kinds of crab apples, 90 kinds of lilacs, and 60 kinds of junipers. The Cary Award Collection trials award-winning varieties of woody trees and shrubs for Vermont's climate (even though the farm is in Zone 5, which precludes testing for Zones 3 and 4).

Self-guided walks take visitors through parts of the Hort Farm, such as a new fern collection. In a display garden not far from the parking area, perennial flowers are nicely labeled and evaluated for value as cut flowers, hardiness, and disease resistance.

The Hort Farm is free and generally open to the public from 8:00 a.m. to 4:00 p.m. Monday through Friday during the growing season. It is closed holidays, during the apple-picking season, during the winter, or if there is no available staff on-site. If you'd like to visit, it is best to call the farm at (802) 658-9166. You may also e-mail Terry Bradshaw at tbradsha@uvm.edu. Docents are available to give you a guided tour if you make arrangements in advance.

The Hort Farm is located on Green Mountain Drive, off Route 7 in South Burlington. For more information go to www.friends ofthehortfarm.org.

Shelburne Farms. This 1400-acre working farm and non-profit environmental learning area is located 5 miles south of Burlington. In the late 1800s Mrs. Lila Vanderbilt Webb and her husband bought 3,800 acres of farmland on Shelburne Point, on the shores of Lake Champlain. The Webbs developed the area and used it as a residence and model farm.

The Webbs hired Frederick Law Olmsted, the father of American landscape architecture and one of the designers of Central Park in New York City, to create a plan for the property. Olmsted's design used landscape as a medium for creating art out of the natural terrain. Instead of straight farm roads, he drew meandering lanes that curved around the contours of the land. He used the long views of Lake Champlain and the mountains of New York State as backdrops for the planned buildings and gardens. He succeeded wonderfully.

The Webbs hired a well-known architect, Robert Robertson, to design the buildings. They spared no expense. Although great mansions are not uncommon in the United States, great barns such as the Farm Barn and the Breeding Barn are truly one of a kind. These structures are huge and architecturally interesting. The Breeding Barn is so large that in the farm's heyday polo matches were sometimes held indoors.

In 1972 the farm became a nonprofit corporation with the mission of cultivating a conservation ethic and teaching steward-ship of natural and agricultural resources. Shelburne Farms has since been designated a National Historic Landmark. The historic home is now a seasonal inn near the water of Lake Champlain. It is around this building that the most interesting flower gardens have been re-created. Lila Webb was an avid gardener and kept excellent records of everything that she had planted. Thus in the 1980s when the garden restoration began, the gardens could be replanted using authentic plant varieties in the original design.

The Grand Allee gardens in front of the inn were designed to encompass the ideas of Gertrude Jekyll, a famous English designer who favored cottage gardens. The flowers are massed by color, starting with cool blues and purples at the ends of long beds and working to the center, where warm reds and yellows dominate. Peak bloom is June through mid-July. There are also 80 feet of peony beds peaking in mid-June. Offspring of Lila Webb's peony called 'Queen Victoria' are still in the garden.

The area known today as the Enchanted Forest was re-created in the early 1990s based on Mrs. Webb's "wild garden." It has meandering paths through wooded areas full of interesting shrubs and a collection of garden statuary.

The farm is open daily from mid-May to mid-October from 9:00 a.m. to 5:30 p.m., offering tours and educational workshops. Cheese and bread are made and sold on the farm. The walking trails are open year-round, weather permitting. Admission is $8 for adults, $6 for seniors, and $5 for children ages three to seventeen. A wagon tour of the property is offered for an additional $3 per person in season, and tea tours of the inn and gardens are offered Tuesday and Thursday at 2:30 p.m. by reservation. Shelburne Farms is located on Bay Road, off Route 7 south of Burlington. For more information visit www.shelburnefarms.org or phone (802) 985-8686.

Shelburne Museum. Each May the Shelburne Museum celebrates the onset of summer with a Lilac Festival. The museum has more than 400 lilacs in 90 different varieties that decorate the grounds. But that collection is just one of many—including plants, art, and folklore—that are housed on the forty-five-acre site just half an hour from Burlington.

The grounds feature six themed gardens in addition to the lilacs and many mature trees. Each garden has a map and excellent labeling, providing the opportunity to learn about gardening in Vermont in periods from the 1790s to the present day.

The Apothecary Garden, sited next to the apothecary shop, holds thirty-three different species of plants, including many you might not know had medicinal uses. The Hat and Fragrance Garden provides scented perennials and herbs, plus dye plants used in decorating women's hats. The Bostwick Garden is a formal garden designed to represent an artist's palette. The Dutton House Kitchen Garden grows thirty-five kinds of vegetables from the 1820s. The Settler's Kitchen Garden grows plants typically found in 1790s Vermont. Lastly, there is Alyssia's Garden, a typical nineteenth-century-style playground. A picket fence surrounds a lawn where children can run free, and flowers are grown around the perimeter.

There is a working merry-go-round and a 220-foot-long steamboat, the *Ticonderoga*, that was transported from Lake Champlain on a rail line built just for the boat. Galleries display fine art and historical artifacts. A beautiful old round barn serves as the welcome center.

The Shelburne Museum is located on Route 7 in Shelburne. It is open May 1 to October 31 daily from 10:00 a.m. to 5:00 p.m. Admission is $24 for adults, $12 for children five to twelve, $14 for children ages thirteen to seventeen, free to children under age five. A family pass for two adults and their children is $58. Admission prices for Vermont residents are roughly half price. For more information visit shelburnemuseum.org or call (802) 985-3346.

Horsford Gardens and Nursery. This is Vermont's oldest nursery, around for well over a hundred years. They have very nice display gardens, including a shade garden under two ancient locust trees, a full-sun perennial garden, three big circles of daylilies and irises, and a shrub border garden. They grow their own stock and have extensive collections of larger trees for sale, including some with 6-inch diameter trunks that they use on landscaping projects.

Horsford Gardens and Nursery are located on Route 7 in Charlotte, 10 miles south Burlington. The gardens are free and open to the public from April 15 to October 31. For more information visit www.horsfordnursery.com or call 802-425-2811.

Central Vermont

Rocky Dale Nursery. Owner Ed Burke bought this established nursery in 2003 and has been improving the already spectacular display gardens. Linked by lawn, a series of garden rooms showcases mature decorative shrubs and trees, many of them unusual, as well as perennial flowers. Cliffs rise dramatically behind the gardens, displaying many native ferns and mosses. Despite its location, the gardens include many Zone 5 plants.

Rocky Dale is located east of Bristol on Route 7. For more information visit www.rockydalegardens.com or call (802) 453-2782.

Southern Vermont

Hildene. This is the home and gardens of Robert Todd Lincoln, the sole child of President Abraham Lincoln to live to adulthood.

Robert Todd Lincoln was an industrialist, the president of the Pullman Porter Company, manufacturers of train cars back when the rails ruled. The Lincoln family used the property as a summer home.

The gardens at Hildene were originally designed by Lincoln's daughter, Jessie, in 1907 as a gift for her mother. The setting for these formal gardens is spectacular, with peaks of the Green Mountains on one side and steep cliffs dropping off to a flat valley some 300 feet below. The formal garden is designed to mimic a Gothic cathedral window: Perennial flowers provide the color of the window "glass," with low privet hedges representing the lead cames. In mid-June up to 1,000 peony blossoms bloom at once.

The kitchen and cutting gardens that supplied the house with flowers and vegetables were restored in 2003. The 500-acre property also has a network of hiking trails that open for snowshoeing and cross-country skiing in winter.

Hildene is in Manchester, south of the village on Route 7A. It is open daily from 9:30 a.m. to 4:30 p.m. Tours of the house are available. Admission is $18 for adults and $5 for children age six and older. For more information call (802) 362-1788 or visit www.hildene.org.

Olallie Daylily Gardens. In August, when daylilies are at their peak, these gardens are heaven for daylily collectors. Owner Chris Darrow is a grandson of George Darrow, a renowned daylily breeder who was a pioneer breeder of tetraploid daylilies in the 1960s. The gardens feature six acres of daylilies of all sizes, colors, and bloom types—all well labeled. Not only that, someone will dig you a division of anything you fancy. Companion perennials are also on sale. Only organic techniques are used in these gardens.

Olallie is found at 129 Augur Hole Road in South Newfane. Visit www.daylilygarden.com for a map, hours, and further directions, or call them at (802) 348-6614.

Eastern Vermont

Cider Hill Gardens. This gem of a garden center in Windsor has terrific display gardens showing off their collection of less-common shade plants, wildflowers, and hostas. It is a naturally beautiful setting with exposed rock and old apple trees. Gary and Sarah Milek also have lovely full-sun gardens: a nice collection of daylilies and peonies and an herb garden with great diversity of plants. Gary's artwork, from original egg tempura paintings to inexpensive prints, features plants and is available to see—or buy—in a gallery on the premises. For directions and information call (802) 674-6825 or visit www.ciderhillvt.com.

Path of Life Sculpture Garden. This is a large, largely open space along the Connecticut River near the Harpoon Brewery off Route 5 in Windsor. It has a maze and a labyrinth, and some lovely sculpture. Open year round, dawn to dusk. Admission $5 by donation.

Marsh-Billings-Rockefeller National Historical Park and Billings Farm and Museum. These two sites are across the street from each other outside of Woodstock. The former is small compared to many national parks (it has just 550 acres) but has a fine formal flower garden typical of the early twentieth century, 20 miles of carriage roads, and a twenty-eight-room mansion that is fit for, well, a Rockefeller.

Marsh-Billings-Rockefeller National Historic Park is the nation's only park dedicated to the educating the public about land stewardship and conservation. The Rockefellers donated the property to the National Park Service. It has the oldest planned and managed forest in the United States.

The formal flower garden is resplendent with flowers all summer long. It is roughly a 75-foot square that is divided in quadrants and punctuated with a fountain at its center. From early bulbs, peonies, and iris to the meadow rue that towers over English tea roses, hollyhocks, dahlias, and lilies, the garden has a constant display of color. All the plants are labeled.

Instrumental in the design of the gardens was Ellen Biddle Shipman, one of the country's first female garden designers who worked on the gardens in 1912 and 1913. She stressed simplicity and privacy in her designs, believing that a garden should be "a place of beauty where one can go to rest and meditate." The gardens have changed since she worked on them, but they are consistent with her goals.

Just across the street is the Billings Farm and Museum, a working farm with an heirloom vegetable garden, a herd of forty milking Jerseys, Southdown sheep, and a museum illustrating every aspect of rural life in the 1890s. The museum offers educational displays and programs of special interest to children and families.

During the summer the Billings Farm and Museum has a kitchen garden with unusual heirloom vegetables. 'Pencil Pod Black' wax beans and 'Wren's Egg' pole beans might grow near 'Green-striped Cushaw' pumpkins or purple 'Vienna' kohlrabi. Never grown a mangel? That's not surprising, but you can see red mangels or perhaps 'Golden Tankard' mangels at the farm. Mangels, grown decades ago as animal feed, are a type of beet. In the spring a limited supply of seed packets are available for sale to visitors. Each year the array of vegetables changes, but most years there are forty different varieties of some eighteen vegetables growing.

Both the Marsh-Billings-Rockefeller Park and the Billings Farm are located on Route 12, just half a mile north of Woodstock. For more information about the park including hours and fees, visit www.nps.gov/mabi or call (802) 457-3368, ext. 22. For information about the farm, visit www.billingsfarm.org or call (802) 457-2355.

Northern Vermont

Trapp Family Lodge. The gardens here are nice, but the view is even better. The lodge is situated outside of Stowe, on the top of the world. Despite its northern location and exposed landscape, the lodge's gardens have some unusual plants, including giant colewort (*Crambe cordifolia*) that blooms dramatically in June with 3-foot flower panicles. Many of the plantings are annuals best seen in summer.

The Trapp Family Lodge gardens are free and open to the public; you'll find the lodge at 700 Trapp Hill Road in Stowe. For more details visit www.trappfamily.com or call (800) 826-7000 or (802) 253-8511.

Cadys Falls Nursery. Wonderful, mature display gardens showcase weeping and unusual conifers, rock garden plants, and lesser-known perennials. Nursery owners Don and Lela Avery have created dozens of small gardens with unusual plants in distinctly different ecological niches, each with a clear identity.

Cadys Falls grows and sells fifteen species of lady's slipper orchids, and the display of showy lady's slippers in mid-June is quite amazing. Other unusual gardens include a sphagnum bog with pitcher plants, a collection of ferns that Don propagates from spore, a water lily garden, and a tufa garden. Tufa is a naturally occurring calcium carbonate rock. Don has drilled holes in the stone, allowing them to grow unusual rock garden plants.

The gardens are a cross between a designer's garden and a collector's garden: Thousands of varieties of plants are clustered in small collections, not in mass plantings. The various collections are nicely hidden by hedges or tall plants. Unlike most garden centers, Cadys Falls grows its own nursery stock and does not bother with the newest introductions in the nursery trade. They are moving toward retirement, so visit the website to see when they are open, which is very limited.

Cadys Falls Nursery is located at 637 Duhamel Road in Morrisville. Visit www.cadysfallsnursery.com or call (802) 888-5559.

Elmore Roots Nursery. This is the place to go for fruit and nut trees, hardy roses, grapes and kiwis, roses, lilacs, and other woody plants that could almost thrive in the Arctic. Elmore Roots is in Zone 3, and owner David Fried's mantra is, "If it will grow in

Elmore, it will grow where you are." This is an orchard and nursery, and as such not as graceful in layout and design as some garden centers listed above, but it is welcoming and comfortable to visit and enables you to see the size and form of mature fruit (and other) trees, shrubs, and vines. A golf cart is available for use by those who can't walk long distances, and nice benches offer shady places to rest. Elmore Roots is the only certified organic tree nursery in the state and one of just a few in New England.

Elmore Roots conducts workshops on pruning, songbird habitats, and other tree-related topics and offers tasting tours of their apples, grapes, and other fruits. You'll find the nursery at 631 Symonds Mill Road, Wolcott. For more information visit www. elmoreroots.com or call 802-888-3305. The nursery is closed on Saturday.

Perennial Pleasures Nursery and Tea Garden. This is the place to go for an English cream tea in a garden that grows over 800 varieties of plants. Located in E. Hardwick, visit www.perennial pleaseures.net for hours, directions, and more. They specialize in tall garden phlox. For more information call (802) 472-5104. Open in gardening season only, and closed Monday.

Final Thoughts

It's easy to get bogged down in gardening, to focus exclusively on improving the soil and planting and weeding. But it's valuable to get away from your home garden from time to time. Take a day off, invite a friend, pack a picnic, and go visit other gardens, public or private. There is so much to learn and to enjoy. Visiting an heirloom garden can be a bit like climbing into a time machine. And Vermont's family-run garden centers—too numerous to list here— are full of knowledgeable and friendly people who love plants.

CHAPTER FOURTEEN

Resources for the Vermont Gardener

Gardening Questions

Master Gardener Helpline

For a quick answer to a gardening question, call the Master Gardener Helpline at (800) 639-2230 or (802) 656-5421. Master Gardeners are on call to provide answers to most gardening questions for the citizens of Vermont, and they confer with University of Vermont Extension personnel if you stump them.

The helpline is generally open Monday through Friday from 9:00 a.m. to noon. In winter the hours are subject to change. You may leave a message and someone will get back to you. You can also e-mail questions anytime through www.uvm.edu/master gardener. That website is full of good information, just click on the Resources link. It has great photos for weed identification, and you can check out the plant hardiness zone map (click on Vermont on the national map for a close-up view).

Insect and Disease Diagnosis

Call the Master Gardener Helpline (see above). The Master Gardener on call will try to help you, but will be glad to forward your sample to the UVM Plant Diagnostic Lab if need be. There is no charge for home gardeners who send samples to the lab through the Master Gardener Helpline.

Continuing Education

Master Gardener Program

The University of Vermont Extension conducts Master Gardener training once per year, with registration each fall for winter classes. If you have a flexible schedule and can commit not only to attending classes but to volunteering afterward, this is a wonderful opportunity. If you would like to become a Master Gardener, go to www.uvm.edu/mastergardener/?Page=become.html, or call (802) 656-9562.

The thirteen-week introductory course, presented via interactive television at many sites around the state, includes all the basics of home horticulture. The instructors are UVM faculty and Vermont horticulture professionals. Topics include botany, vegetables, turf and weeds, entomology, plant pathology, soils, woody ornamentals, perennials and annuals, introduction to landscape design or sustainable landscaping, applied pest management, UVM Extension volunteering, and invasive plant control.

The course takes thirteen weeks, starting in early February and running until the end of April. Starting in 2016, it will be an interactive online course meeting Tuesday evenings from 6:15 to 9:15. Tuition for the course is $395. The *Master Gardener Training Handbook* and instructors materials (required) are an additional $50, but free if you want to download it yourself. Call (802) 656-9562 for details. Some scholarships are available. To receive your Vermont Master Gardener certificate, you must complete a volunteer internship of forty hours in addition to the basic course, and then twenty hours each year you are active. Graduates (Master Gardener interns) partner with certified Master Gardeners on local projects. The Master Gardener program is also starting a four-week Master Composter mini-course.

Soil Testing

Before you start your first garden, and every three or four years thereafter, it's a good idea to have your soil tested. University of Vermont Extension offers this service for $14, which includes measures of important minerals, organic matter, micronutrients, and more. If you are growing vegetables, pay an extra $10 at least once to see if there is lead, cadmium, or other heavy metals in your vegetable garden soil. Prices are subject to change.

To get a soil testing kit, download the form and instructions and mail the form and a soil sample in a plastic baggie.

You may also get soil test kits from the offices of UVM Extension or the Natural Resources Conservation Service (NRCS) in your county. There are eleven NRCS offices around Vermont.

Books

Every gardener needs books as references. Here are my recommendations—look through these and decide which you need. A few are pretty expensive, but you can encourage your library to get them. I've put an asterisk next to the ones everyone should have, while the others are for gardeners with specific interests. Some of these are out of print, but you can get them by calling your local used book dealer. Also note: Many of these authors have written several books, and generally if one is good, all are good.

Armitage, Allan. *Armitage's Garden Perennials: A Garden Encyclopedia*. This species-by-species book includes a dozen different cultivars of each of the flowers illustrated with excellent photos.

Barnes and Noble Books. *Botanica: The Illustrated Encyclopedia of Over 10,000 Garden Plants and How to Cultivate Them*. One paragraph and a photo for most common and many uncommon plants.

*Cebenko, Jill Jesiolowski, and Deborah L. Martin, eds. *Insect, Disease & Weed I.D. Guide: Find-It-Fast Organic Solutions for Your Garden*. This wonderful book not only identifies problems but also provides life cycles and solutions. Excellent. Out of print, but readily available.

*Cruso, Thalassa. *Making Things Grow: A Practical Guide for the Indoor Gardener*. The best book I've seen about growing houseplants. Currently out of print, but worth looking for secondhand.

Deppe, Carol. *The Tao of Vegetable Gardening: Cultivating Tomatoes, Greens, Peas, Beans, Squash, Joy, and Serenity*. The title says it all! Excellent, even for experienced gardeners.

Dirr, Michael. *Dirr's Encyclopedia of Trees & Shrubs*. The perfect companion to his book listed next, it is full of excellent photos. It's a great book to thumb through before going to the plant nursery.

Dirr, Michael. *Manual of Woody Landscape Plants: Their Identification, Ornamental Characteristics, Culture, Propagation and Uses*. This is my bible for woody plants. Dirr is the most knowledgeable author about trees. He is also highly opinionated. His book is an $80 paperback with 1,200 pages of useful information. Your local library should have it or be able to get it through interlibrary loan.

*Disabato-Aust, Tracy. *The Well-Tended Perennial Garden: Planting and Pruning Techniques*. This is a must-have because it will tell you when and how to prune your perennials for better vigor—and how to get them to bloom more than once a season.

Eddison, Sydney. *The Gardener's Palette: Creating Color in the Garden*. This explains how colors work and how to combine them. Great design tips.

Evans, Trevor. *Forest Trees of Vermont.* Spiral-bound and water-resistant pages. It has QR codes you can scan with your smart phone, too, to get even more info from the USDA. Lots of photos. Excellent resource, not too technical.

Hayward, Gordon. *Stone in the Garden: Inspiring Designs and Practical Projects.* Hayward is a Vermont-based garden designer whose books are all excellent. This one is for anyone who needs to build a wall or a walk.

Hill, Lewis, and Nancy Hill. *The Flower Gardener's Bible.* Written by Vermonters who were in the nursery business for fifty-plus years; all their books are excellent. This starts with the soil, covers design issues, and includes a plant-by-plant directory with pictures.

Hodgson, Larry. *Annuals for Every Purpose: Choosing the Right Plants for Your Conditions, Your Garden, and Your Taste.* There are too many annuals to know them all, but this guy seems to. A Rodale book, so it has an organic slant to flower care.

*Homeyer, Henry. *Notes from the Garden: Reflections and Observations of an Organic Gardener.* This is a month-by-month guide to what I do in my own gardens, along with interviews of interesting gardeners. Selected as one of the best gardening books of 2002 by the *Christian Science Monitor*, so I'm not just bragging! A follow-up book of the same sort came out in 2011: Organic Gardening (not just) in the Northeast: A Hands-on Month by Month Guide. The best of my newspaper and magazine articles collected over a 10-year period.

Messervy, Julie Moir. *The Inward Garden: Creating a Place of Beauty and Meaning.* An excellent book to help you understand what type of garden suits you best and how to create it. She has written several other good design books.

Ogren, Thomas. *Allergy-Free Gardening: The Revolutionary Guide to Healthy Landscaping.* Useful for anyone who suffers from pollen allergies.

Pellet, Norman. *Native Shrubs and Vines for Northern New England Landscapes.* This book is available from the Friends of the Horticulture Farm at UVM. To order call (802) 864-3073 or visit www.uvm.edu/~hortfarm/.

Pellet, Norman, and Mark Starrett. Landscape Plants for Vermont. Published by UVM Extension and available from the Vermont Master Gardeners, this has good plants for Vermont organized by growing characteristics. To order call (800) 639-2230 or go to www.uvm.edu/mastergardener/LPV2002/LPV.htm.

*Reich, Lee. *The Pruning Book.* This is the best book on pruning I've seen. It has lots of good illustrations, straightforward explanations, and species-specific information for trees, shrubs, and vines.

*Smith, Edward. *The Vegetable Gardener's Bible.* This has everything you need to know to be a good organic vegetable gardener. If you wish to grow vegetables in containers, his book *Incredible Vegetables from Self-Watering Containers* is excellent.

Still, Steven. *Manual of Herbaceous Ornamental Plants.* More than 800 pages of text with growing tips, hardiness zones, soil preferences, and descriptions of specific cultivars. This is the book I reach for most often, though it has only forty-seven pages of small color photos—eight per page—in the back. For the serious gardener.

*Walliser, Jessica. *Good Bug, Bad Bug: Who's Who, What They Do, and How to Manage Them Organically*. Spiral-bound with water-resistant pages; take this in the garden to ID your bugs. Everyone should have it.

Seed, Equipment, and Plant Suppliers

These are a few of the catalogs that I order from and have always been pleased with the quality of their goods. The four asterisked companies are my mainstays, but I use the others for specialty items.

Baker Creek Heirloom Seeds. These folks have a great variety of heirloom seeds—things you can't find elsewhere. The company was started in 1997 by a seventeen-year-old! (417) 924-8917; www.rareseeds.com. They are no longer taking orders by phone.

Brent and Becky's Bulbs. A nice family-run business. Excellent selection, excellent bulbs, and a limited number of hard-to-find perennials. (877) 661-2852; www.https://brentandbeckysbulbs.com.

The Cook's Garden. Unusual vegetable seeds, including 'Kwintus' pole beans, the best of all beans. Started by Vermonters and now owned by Burpee Seeds. (800) 457-9703; www.cooks garden.com.

***Fedco Seeds.** A Maine cooperative that supplies seeds, equipment, bare-root trees in season, seed potatoes, and bulbs. Prices are excellent, as is service. (207) 873-7333; www.fedcoseeds.com. They do not accept phone orders, but they will answer questions.

***Gardener's Supply.** An employee-owned company in Burlington that sells plants, seeds, equipment, books, and more at their retail outlets in Burlington and Williston. Their catalog has lots of good things (though not everything they have at the stores). (800) 427-3363; www.gardeners.com.

Gardens Alive. This specialty catalog provides supplies for organic gardeners, with everything from insecticidal soaps and bio-fungicides to red worms and composters. (513) 354-1482; www. gardensalive.com.

Growers Supply. A business offering greenhouses and other supplies. (800) 476-9715; www.growerssupply.com.

*High Mowing Seeds. This Vermont-based company is one of the very few who sell only organic seeds. They sell varieties that do well in cold climates like ours, and they provide information to gardeners who want to save seeds. (802) 472-6174; www.high mowingseeds.com.

Hudson Valley Seed Library. Located in upstate New York, this is the newest seed company, and one that is certified organic. They grow heirloom and open-pollinated plants, and will actually buy seeds from you, if you follow their directions. www.seed library.org.

*Johnny's Selected Seeds. A Maine-based company that really works hard at breeding and testing plants that do well in our climate. They have developed many award-winning varieties and have an incredibly diverse catalog. Their catalog offers great advice on each plant variety. (877) 564-6697; www.johnnyseeds.com.

Lee Valley Tools. Very good tools at very good prices. I keep garden records in a ten-year gardener's journal the company sells, which makes record keeping easy. (800) 871-8158; www.leevalley. com.

McClure & Zimmerman. Extensive collection of unusual bulbs. (800) 546-4053; www.mzbulb.com.

New England Wild Flower Society. A great source for wildflowers, including rare ones. A visit to their headquarters, the Garden in the Woods in Framingham, Massachusetts, is a great spring field trip. (508) 877-7630; www.newfs.org.

Nichols Garden Nursery. Lots of unusual varieties, heirlooms. 800-422-3985; www.nicholsgardennursery.com.

OESCO, Inc. This is a great source for tools you can't find elsewhere, and at reasonable prices. I get all my pruning and grafting supplies from them. (800)634-5557; www.oescoinc.com.

Peace Seeds. Small, family-run seed company. Alan is a serious plant breeder who has developed many seed varieties. The only seed company that acknowledges Bob Dylan, Joan Baez, and The Grateful Dead on its website. www.peaceseeds.com.

Renee's Garden Seeds. Gourmet vegetables, kitchen herbs, and cottage-garden flowers. The seed packets are rich with growing information. (888) 800-7228; www.reneesgarden.com.

Seeds of Change. All certified-organic seeds. (888) 762-7333; www.seedsofchange.com.

Sprinkler Warehouse. Offering everything needed by gardeners and farmers who want to set up drip irrigation systems. (855) 290-0815; www.sprinklerwarehouse.com.

Organizations and Events

Branch Out Burlington. This organization organizes community tree-planting events, hosts local guided tree walks, manages the Burlington Community Tree Nursery, and sponsors both educational seminars and the Awesome Tree Contest. Everyone is welcome at their meetings. Learn more at www.branchoutburlington. org. If you are interested in having a tree in front of your house and are willing to learn about tree care and water your tree, please get in touch with them through their website.

The Awesome Tree Contest is an annual event that allows people to submit nominations for their favorite trees. The five different categories of trees are the Tallest, Widest, Most Unusual Variety, Tree with a Story, and Picture Perfect. The contest runs for the months of August and September. The rules are pretty simple. All nominated trees must be within Burlington city limits and no tree can win the same category twice.

Friends of the Horticulture Farm. This is an organization that supports the University of Vermont Horticultural Research Center ("the Hort Farm") in all its activities and offers educational opportunities to its members. By joining the Friends of the Hort Farm ($25 for an individual, $35 for a family), you will obtain a bimonthly newsletter that provides information on upcoming classes and events at the Hort Farm and research results on plants being tested (such as Dr. Mark Starrett's evaluation of the berries on winterberry shrubs). Membership in the Friends of the Hort Farm also includes discounts on their classes, the New England Wild Flower Society Symposium each year, and entry to the Members' Preview at the annual benefit plant sale held at the farm in late July. To join call (802) 864-3073 or go to www .friendsofthehortfarm.org.

Hardy Plants Club of Vermont. This is a group of about 200 plant people, from dedicated amateurs to professional horticulturists and professors. The club has eight to ten meetings per year: trips, lectures, open gardens. Membership is $10 a year. To join, e-mail your interest to hardyplantclubvt@gmail.com. I'm a member, and I recommend joining because, among other things, you will get to see some very wonderful gardens that are not open to the public and meet people who know a tremendous amount about plants. For more info go to hardyplantclubvt.blogspot.com.

Local garden clubs. Join your local club, and you can learn something from the members and from the speakers most clubs invite. Many local clubs sponsor garden tours of their members' gardens each summer, so you can see what grows well in your town. Most garden tours are open to the public. Take several each year if you wish!

Northeast Organic Farmers Association. Started in 1971, this is an organization of farmers and gardeners who believe in growing without chemicals. The annual winter conference, held in February, is a bit like traveling back in time to the 1960s: It is full of back-to-the-earth types who revere the earth and are anxious to do their bit to make it better. In addition to a nationally known keynote speaker, the conference offers two days of workshops useful for beginner or old-timer: keeping bees, starting a vineyard, working with herbs, growing apples organically, and more. Definitely fun! NOFA also conducts a series of summer workshops.

To join or to learn more, go to nofavt.org or call (802) 434-4122. Membership is $30 a year and includes a quarterly magazine, reduced prices on workshops, and the opportunity to buy soil amendments through their bulk order program.

The Vermont Flower Show. Held every other year in early spring, this show is a great chance to hear knowledgeable speakers talk about specific aspects of gardening in Vermont. It is also a great way to get inundated by the smells and sights of spring—thousands of forced bulbs, flowers, and trees grace the hall. A highlight for kids—big and little—is the exhibit of model trains running though a well-landscaped scene. For more information go to http://green worksvermont.org. The show is sponsored by the Vermont Association of Professional Horticulturists. It is currently being held at Champlain Valley Exposition, Essex Junction, though that can change.

Glossary

annual: Any plant that lives its life in one year and then dies when winter comes. Lettuce, marigolds, and crabgrass are annuals. Some flowers called annuals in Vermont may be perennials in the tropics.

Azomite: A commercially available rock powder that offers many minerals not found in fertilizers.

biennial: Any plant that lives just two years, then dies. Flowering occurs in the second year. Foxgloves, parsley, and carrots are examples.

branch collar: A swollen area, usually wrinkled, where a branch meets the trunk or a larger branch. It is the area where healing takes place when a branch is pruned, and it should not be removed.

brashed: To have removed all lower branches on a tree trunk, particularly those of pine trees.

brassica: This is the name of a family of vegetables including broccoli, cabbage, Brussels sprouts, kohlrabi, rutabagas, and turnips. These are also referred to as cruciferous vegetables.

cambium layer: A layer of cells in plants that is responsible for thickening of the stems.

canes: Stems, particularly for multistemmed shrubs, berries, and roses.

chemical fertilizer: Fertilizer manufactured using petroleum products and chemicals.

clay: Soil that is composed of extremely fine rock particles. Clay retains water, and clay soil is commonly referred to as heavy soil.

corn gluten: A corn product sold to prevent annual weed seeds from germinating. It must be applied in the early spring before seeds germinate. Contains 10 percent nitrogen.

crown: The growing point of grasses, asparagus, and strawberries.

cultivar: A named variety of a plant that has been identified as having specific characteristics. 'Crimson King', for example, is a cultivar or variety of Norway maple that has purple leaves—most other Norway maples have green leaves.

damping-off: A fungal disease that results in young seedlings falling over and collapsing. Once it affects a plant, there is little hope for recovery.

day-neutral: A term indicating that production of flowers or fruit is not related to the seasonal changes in the length of day. Most plants do react to changes in day length.

deadhead: To cut off or remove flower heads.

deciduous: Any tree or shrub that loses its leaves in winter.

dolomitic limestone: This is the commonly found type, which contains magnesium in addition to calcium. It is used to make soils less acidic.

double flowers: Flowers with several sets of petals, as opposed to single flowers that just have one set of petals. Peonies and roses, for example, come as either single or double.

fungus/fungi: A parasitic plant that lacks chlorophyll and leaves, true stems, and roots and that reproduces by spores. Both beneficial and disease-causing types occur, both in the soil and on leaf surfaces. Powdery mildew, late blight, and botrytis are disease-causing fungi, while mycorrhizal fungi are very beneficial.

genetically modified organisms (GMOs): Organisms that scientists have developed in a lab by introducing genes from one species into another to confer special characteristics. For example, a gene from a bacterium has been introduced into a corn plant to produce a protein that is poisonous to insects. Once developed, the seeds are patented and legally may not be saved from year to year.

glacial till: Residue deposited by glaciers, usually containing sand and rocks.

hardening off: The process of acclimatizing plants started indoors to the direct sun and to the drying effects of the wind.

hips: Seedpods of roses.

humus: A chemically complex organic material that results from the breakdown of raw organic matter by microorganisms. It is a key ingredient in all good soils, and one that makes them dark in color.

hybrid: A plant that is the result of intentional breeding, the crossing of two plants with different genetic material. Seeds saved from hybrids will not usually breed true.

hydroponics: The process of growing plants in water fortified with nutrients.

lean soil: A soil poor in nitrogen, such as an un-amended sandy soil.

loam: A soil type consisting of a good mixture of sand, silt, and clay.

macronutrients: Carbon, hydrogen, nitrogen, phosphorus, and potassium combine to make up the bulk of plants' bodies. All five elements are essential for plant growth and survival.

micronutrients: Elements that are important in very small amounts for the proper functioning of biological systems.

nematodes: Small unsegmented worms found in all soils. They may be beneficial or parasitic.

nitrogen fixation: The process of taking nitrogen from the air and converting it to a form usable by plants. This is done by a few species of soil bacteria that normally reside in the roots of legumes, or bean-family plants.

organic fertilizer: Fertilizer made from natural ingredients, such as the bodies and by-products of plants and animals, and naturally occurring minerals.

organic matter: Material made by plants and animals. Leaves, manure, and seashells, for example.

pathogen: A disease-causing agent such as a bacteria, virus, or fungus.

peat moss: An organic soil additive harvested from bogs. It is quite acidic. It is commonly used to keep potting mixes from compacting and to retain water. It has very little nutritional value for plants.

pelletized seeds: Seeds coated with a thin layer of clay to increase their size and ability to be handled for planting. Carrot seeds are commonly offered in pelletized form.

perennial: Any plant that comes back and lives year after year. In Vermont perennial flowers go dormant in fall, their above-ground portions die off, and the plants regrow in spring. Peonies, delphinium, and rhubarb are examples.

perlite: A light, fluffy material formed by heating perlite rock until it pops like popcorn. It is an inert ingredient in many planting or starting mixes. It increases water retention and aeration of soil mixes. It looks like Styrofoam.

pH: See soil pH.

pollen-free: A term used for hybrid flowers that have been bred to produce no pollen. Pollen is usually a fine yellow dust, and it can stain tablecloths.

rock powder: Finely ground rock dust that some gardeners believe adds micronutrients and minerals that contribute to plant vigor. Ask for 200 screen rock dust if buying it at a quarry. Azomite is a bagged rock powder.

root hairs: Very fine extensions of roots that do the most important work of roots: absorbing water and nutrients. They are so small you cannot see them with the naked eye.

root suckers: Shoots or stems that grow from the roots of an established woody plant. Lilacs and apples commonly send up root suckers.

scapes: Leafless flower stems. Daylily blossoms, for example, grow on scapes that can be anywhere from 1 to 5 feet in length.

silt: Soil made of medium-sized mineral particles. It is often deposited by streams.

single flowers: Those flowers that have just a single concentric ring of petals.

soil pH: A measure of acidity or alkalinity. It is a scale from 1 to 14, with 7 being neutral; as numbers get lower, they indicate more acidic conditions. It is a logarithmic scale, so a pH of 5 is 10 times more acidic than a pH of 6. Most plants do best in the range of 6 to 6.8.

spores: Produced by fungi, they are equivalent to seeds in green plants.

stomata: Pores found on the underside of leaves. They are the sites where plants take in carbon dioxide from the atmosphere and give off oxygen and water.

sweet soil: Alkaline soil, or anything with a pH above 7. Limestone and wood ashes sweeten acidic soil, making it less acidic.

symbiotic relationship: One in which both organisms benefit. Mycorrhizal fungi, for example, share soil minerals with tree roots and obtain excess sugars exuded by the roots in return.

texture: The particular blend of soil you have, which depends on the mixture of sand, silt, and clay present.

tilth: How well a soil holds water and allows air to pass through it. "Good tilth" describes a soil that is light and fluffy.

top-dressing: A layer of compost, fertilizer, or manure spread on the soil surface near a plant to enrich the soil.

transpiration: The giving off of water vapor from the leaves of plants. Roughly equivalent to sweating (in people). Transpiration pulls up water and nutrients from the soil.

trunk flare: The base of a tree where roots flare out and appear to snake across the ground a little before disappearing beneath the surface.

variety: A cultivar. Plants that have been identified as having specific characteristics are called varieties or cultivars. Macintosh is a variety of apple.

vermiculite: A substance used to keep a planting medium light and fluffy when potting plants or starting seedlings. It is heat-expanded mica that holds water, releasing it to plants as needed.

water table: This indicates at what level water remains in the ground. In summer the water table might be 4 feet below the surface, but in spring there might be standing water just a foot below the surface if drainage is poor.

zones: Referring to USDA Hardiness Zones that indicate how cold it gets during an average winter. Zone 3 is minus 30 to 40 degrees; Zone 4 is minus 20 to 30 degrees; Zone 5 is minus 10 to 20 degrees. These zones determine what perennial and woody plants you can select for your garden.

Index

grubs, 155
Guenther, Bill, 160

H
hardening off, 67
hardiness zone map, 23
hardiness zones, 22
Hardy Plants Club of
    Vermont, 221
Harper, Wendy Sue, 3, 4,
    7, 17
Hazelrigg, Ann, 182, 185
hedge maple, 137
heirloom seeds, 61
hemlock wooly adelgid, 197
highbush blueberry, 142, 169
Hildene, 206
Hill, Lewis, 30
hoes, 174
Honigford, Geo, 74
hoop house, 32
hoop house (how to build), 33
horseradish, 71
Horsford Gardens and
    Nursery, 206
hoses, 180
hostas, 119
hot boxes, 36
humus, 5
hybrid seeds, 61
hydrangeas, 138
hydrogen, 12
I
impatiens, 105
integrated pest management
    (IPM), 161, 184
invasive plants, 158–169
    alternatives for, 167

biological controls, 163
chemical controls for
    organic gardeners, 166
mechanical controls, 162
Vermont official list of
    prohibited invasive
    plants, 159
Iresine, 98
iron, 13

J
Jack-in-the-pulpit, 122
Japanese beetles, 194
Japanese red maple, 168

K
Kalm St. Johnswort, 141
Kentucky bluegrass, 149
Korean mountain ash, 135
Krieg, Liz, 88–89, 91, 97–98

L
large fothergilla, 168
larkspur, 99
Latin names, 96
lavender, 120
lawns, 144–157
    compaction, 148
    diseases, 154
    fall care, 156
    grass clippings, 154
    mowers, 152
    mowing, 152, 157
    organic, 147
    overseeding, 147
    pests, 154
    seed varieties, 149
    shady, 150

U

University of Vermont
 Extension Master Gardener
 Helpline, 212
University of Vermont
 Extension Master Gardener
 Program, 213
University of Vermont
 Horticultural Research
 Center, 202

V

vegetable gardens, 54–77
 good plant varieties for
 Vermont, 69
 planting, 60
 planting tips, 69
 raised beds, 59
 size, 55
 starting from scratch, 54
 starting seedlings
 indoors, 62
 sun requirements, 55
 thinning seedlings, 74
 weeding, 68
Vermont Flower Show,
 The, 222

Virginia bluebells, 118
voles, 200

W

water (conservation), 47
watering cans, 46, 179
watering techniques, 43
watering wand, 180
watering wands, 46
water needs of plants, 41
water (when to), 41, 50
weather records for
 Vermont, 24
weeding tools, 175
wheelbarrows, 178
white pine, 142
wild bleeding heart, 119
wildflowers, 121
winter aconite, 122
winterberry, 142
wood ashes, 17
woodchucks, 199

Z

zinc, 13
zinnias, 97, 98, 99

About the Author

Henry Homeyer is a lifetime organic gardener with more than fifty years of experience and a University of New Hampshire Cooperative Extension Master Gardener. He writes a weekly gardening column for newspapers around New England and was the Vermont/New Hampshire Associate Editor for *People, Places, and Plants* magazine for 10 years. He is a regular commentator on Vermont and New Hampshire Public Radio and the author of four gardening books. His *Notes from the Garden: Reflections and Observations of an Organic Gardener* was selected as one of the best gardening books of 2002 by the *Christian Science Monitor*. He has taught gardening classes at Granite State College and Lebanon College.